feedback

*For my boys Sam and Zach*

# feedback

## The HINGE That Joins Teaching & Learning

## jane e. **pollock**

**CORWIN**
A SAGE Company

## CORWIN
A SAGE Company

FOR INFORMATION:

Corwin

A SAGE Company

2455 Teller Road

Thousand Oaks, California 91320

(800) 233-9936

Fax: (800) 417-2466

www.corwin.com

SAGE Publications Ltd.

1 Oliver's Yard

55 City Road

London EC1Y 1SP

United Kingdom

SAGE Publications India Pvt. Ltd.

B 1/I 1 Mohan Cooperative Industrial Area

Mathura Road, New Delhi 110 044

India

SAGE Publications Asia-Pacific Pte. Ltd.

33 Pekin Street #02-01

Far East Square

Singapore 048763

Acquisitions Editor:   Arnis Burvikovs

Associate Editor:   Desirée A. Bartlett

Editorial Assistant:   Kimberly Greenberg

Production Editor:   Cassandra Margaret Seibel

Copy Editor:   Trey Thoelcke

Typesetter:   C&M Digitals (P) Ltd.

Proofreader:   Jenifer Kooiman

Indexer:   Diggs Publishing Services

Cover Designer:   Scott Van Atta

Permissions Editor:   Adele Hutchinson

Printed in the United States of America

*Library of Congress Cataloging-in-Publication Data*

Pollock, Jane E., 1958–

Feedback: the hinge that joins teaching and learning/Jane Pollock.

p. cm.

Includes bibliographical references and index.

ISBN 978-1-4129-9743-0 (pbk.)

1. Teacher-student relationships.
2. Communication in education.
3. Feedback (Psychology) I. Title.

LB1033.P64 2012

371.102'2—dc23          2011036338

SUSTAINABLE FORESTRY INITIATIVE
Certified Chain of Custody
Promoting Sustainable Forestry
www.sfiprogram.org
SFI-01268

SFI label applies to text stock

11 12 13 14 15 10 9 8 7 6 5 4 3 2 1

# CONTENTS

# PREFACE

Ben Boggs, a biology teacher in Tennessee, tells me that he thinks most teachers today are frustrated with the very same issue: the unmotivated students in every class. Sounding a bit discouraged, he observes that there seem to be about five students in any class any day just not willing to engage in the lesson even though they have the ability. Engagement means achievement, he says.

Adrienne Braxton, an elementary teacher in Kentucky, comments that she used to spend so much time encouraging students to participate that she felt like she barely had time to teach. "Honestly, I felt as though I tried everything to get students to take out their materials, get focused and participate, and still some of the students were acting disengaged."

Darlene Markle, a middle school principal in Wisconsin, tells me that her staff has read, workshopped, and implemented *everything.* Two years ago we spoke about it and she told me she believed she could do just about anything as a principal, but felt stymied when observing hard-working teachers in classrooms facing a number of students who just did not seem to care enough about the lessons to do assignments or do them well. Teachers worked harder, students may even have worked harder, but any day in any classroom in their building you could find some middle school students who disengaged during the lesson.

Some students seem uninspired by daily instruction, even though they have access to better technology, facilities, and materials than every generation of children before them. Teachers at all grade levels and across subject areas comment with dismay that some students choose not to participate in the learning.

During my career, I have spent much of my time working side-by-side with teachers as they plan instruction and with principals observing and giving feedback to teachers about improving learning. Teachers can get remarkably enthusiastic about trying new techniques, which makes the work fun as well as satisfying. But when I started to spend more time in classrooms with the teachers observing their delivery of the lessons we had planned, I began to notice that teachers used the new techniques we talked about and planned for in the lesson, but not all of the students used them. Some students did, but some did not.

Take a basic example like using a graphic organizer. In a history class, the teacher projected words on the board and asked students to work together to draw a flowchart connecting the vocabulary. In a class of twenty-eight students, one student did not even take out a piece of paper. After about three minutes, two students stopped writing but did not disrupt any other students. A student quietly put her head on her desk. In five minutes, three other students had attempted to fill in the organizer, but did not complete the task. They sat in silence. The teacher was busy. Having taken attendance, he walked over to one pair of students, intending, I believe, to make a quick tour of the class, but he stopped to help them. Noting the time, the teacher returned to the front of the room to talk about the words while drawing the flowchart on the board. Most of the students copied what he wrote on the board, or added to their own charts. The five or six students never really became engaged, but never disrupted the class; they just stared ahead, watching the teacher.

This book is about how to change engagement in classrooms like this one. A month after I watched that history class and worked with the teacher on techniques to engage students, I observed again. Every student participated from bell to bell. Ask the teacher and he will tell you that it was a challenge for him to change a few of his teaching habits, but it was worth it to see students be more interactive in class and perform better on assignments and assessments.

As I observed teachers planning, teachers teaching, supervisors observing, and learners learning, I kept asking myself whether there was a single criterion common to all of them that could literally open a floodgate of learning. And, if so, could we replicate it at any level, in any subject area, and in fact, any time a person wanted to learn something new or learn better? Unlike other best practices books or reports about reform, this book draws upon publications in other fields where becoming aware of and changing a single factor results in sustained gains or improvements.

Many of us have read from the genre of books that includes *The Tipping Point,* by Malcolm Gladwell (2002), but they did not help us explain increasing student performance in schools, because a bottom line in business is not the same as personal achievement in schools. In business, the term *tipping point* is used to indicate a situation or episode that dramatically increases a product sale. Stories about Pet Rocks, Hush Puppies suede shoes, Beanie Babies, and the Boston Red Sox winning the World Series are tales of how little things can make big things happen. In schools, little things should be able to make big things happen, too.

Research shows that the factor to advance student engagement and achievement is not just teaching, nor just learning, but interlocking the two. A hinge is the device that allows two sides to swing relative to each other, and feedback seems to be a hinge that allows for the transfer of information from the teacher to the student and back to the teacher again. If we look at learning research, we find that feedback connects students to teachers in a way that acts as a hinge, and the result is accelerated productivity and increased achievement.

The hinge factor to improving student learning in schools is feedback, and in this book I describe why I think we missed it at first when searching for school reform solutions, but now how we can change practices immediately. When we address feedback as a strategy that teachers can teach students to use, student engagement increases and so does student achievement.

# ACKNOWLEDGMENTS

Corwin would like to thank the following individuals for taking the time to provide their editorial insight:

Peter Dillon, Superintendent of Schools
Berkshire Hills Regional School District
Stockbridge, MA

Catherine Duffy, English Department Chairperson
Three Village Central School District
Stony Brook, NY

Kathleen Hwang, Principal
Sanders Corner Elementary School
Ashburn, VA

Steve Knobl, Principal
Gulf High School
New Port Richey, FL

Neil MacNeill, Principal
Ellenbrook Primary School
Ellenbrook, Western Australia

Melanie Mares Sainz, Academic Coach
Lowndes Middle School
Valdosta, GA

Karen L. Tichy, Associate Superintendent
    for Instruction and Special Education
Administrator, Department of Special Education
    and St. Mary's Special Services
Catholic Education Office, Archdiocese
    of Saint Louis, Saint Louis, MO

# HINGES
# IN ACTION

**Chapter 2**

A good goal(s) is key. The goal is the target for performance; feedback is information about where you stand in relation to the goal and how to improve.

**Chapter 3**

Interacting with the goal(s) produces positive results. When you determine where you stand in relation to a goal(s), you become motivated to seek help or information. In class, a student has the opportunity to receive feedback from the teacher, but also can learn to self-regulate.

**Chapter 4**

Peer discussion allows students to seek feedback for clarification and to generate questions. Peer discussion can also motivate students to practice producing useful feedback.

**Chapter 5**

Ongoing assessment during instruction, or formative assessment, offers the student an opportunity to increase performance methodically, maximizing efficiency. Documenting formative assessment gives the teacher a reliable record of all students' performances to increase the possibility of systematically providing instructional opportunities for every student.

**Chapter 6**

Any performer can benefit from feedback. Because teachers focus on providing feedback opportunities for students, they may not realize how powerful feedback can shift their own teaching and assessing from skillful to outstanding.

# ABOUT THE AUTHOR

**Jane E. Pollock,** PhD, Learning Horizon, Inc., specializes in teaching and supervising learning. She consults long-term with schools worldwide to improve student learning and teaching practices. She is the author of *Improving Student Learning One Teacher at a Time* (2007) and the coauthor of *Dimensions of Learning Teacher and Training Manuals* (1996); *Assessment, Grading and Record Keeping* (1999); *Classroom Instruction That Works* (2001); *Improving Student Learning One Principal at a Time* (2009); and *Improving Student Learning by Minding the Gap* (2012). She is an adjunct faculty member for various universities in the United States. A native of Caracas, Venezuela, Dr. Pollock earned degrees at the University of Colorado and Duke University. She can be reached at her website, www.improvestudentlearning .com, or by e-mail at learninghorizon@msn.com.

# CHAPTER ONE

# THE HINGE FACTOR: FEEDBACK

---

I n the 1990s, Arthur Agatston, a cardiologist, identified a hinge factor that irrevocably changed his patients' lives. In the book, *The South Beach Diet* (2003), Agatston describes how his seemingly obvious epiphany that heart-healthy persons tend to be slimmer than his patients who battle heart disease led him to find a way to be slim without following a typical low-calorie diet. Previously Agatston and his patients were unable to successfully lose weight because most diets reduced food intake, caused unhealthy metabolism shifts, and resulted in subsequent weight gain. Low-calorie diets exacerbated their heart-related blood chemistry results. Agatston discovered that the hinge factor for balancing blood chemistry was reducing cravings for certain types of foods, which in turn led to losing unwanted weight. People who intentionally reduced cravings ate, as he described, *heart healthy.* By eating better, patients' cardiology results improved, and they became slimmer.

Agatston argues that one should not try to lose weight. Instead, the South Beach diet provides a protocol for learning how to eat to manage cravings and Agatston provides examples to address many types. His patients, who became aware of the single issue, cravings, conscientiously changed their habits to become heart healthy, and in the process lost weight.

## MANAGING FEEDBACK

Can we make an analogy between a diet example and finding a way to improve student learning, especially for unmotivated or disengaged students?

Managing cravings by increasing eating challenged the prevailing notion that dieters need to reduce food intake. To make the analogy, there would have to be some factor in the science of learning that challenged the conventional wisdom.

More engaged learners achieve better, and to reach goals an observer can see that engaged learners actively seek feedback. In a very subtle way, this challenges the prevailing notion that only the teacher can provide timely and frequent feedback to students. Because higher achieving students have learned to seek feedback, that action also keeps them engaged throughout lessons. The unmotivated or disengaged learner could learn techniques to seek feedback that would, in turn, keep them more engaged in class, resulting in higher achievement.

Just as most dieters were unaware of managing cravings, I find that many students are unaware of tactics to seek feedback. When they learn to use simple tools to seek feedback about their progress, they become as motivated as any other student, engaged in lessons, and are able to perform as self-regulated learners.

### PAUSE TO REFLECT

The prevailing notion is that the teacher gives the feedback to the student. Can a student learn to receive feedback from self and others to be productive in school?

## RESEARCH ON FEEDBACK

In 2001, I coauthored a book about instructional strategies titled *Classroom Instruction That Works* (Marzano, Pickering, & Pollock, 2001). We posited that teachers at any grade level in any subject area could significantly improve learning if they deliberately taught students to use high-yield strategies in order to retain knowledge better, or learn better. One of the strategies, setting goals and providing feedback, showed a strong effect on learning ($d = 0.61$, or a 23 percentile point gain, considered to be very high) (p. 7).

When we think of feedback, we naturally think about assessment of progress. In our daily lives, we receive feedback about our performance on desired goals that we can use to improve ourselves. Feedback tied to a criterion or goal also clarifies relevant prospects for learning more information or for acting. That action intends to improve outcomes and as a result, provides the opportunity for a newly advanced goal.

Feedback can be the hinge factor for improving student learning, but there might be at least two reasons why we have not recognized it before. First, most classroom feedback has intentionally been directed from the teacher to the student, largely based on a behaviorist definition of feedback, intended mostly as assessment of student progress. Teachers evaluate how well students perform on tasks such as classwork, homework, or tests and communicate that to the students. When teachers are asked to increase feedback to students, they often respond that they are already taxed for time and are giving as much feedback as they can possibly give. The techniques this book suggests are primarily intended for students to use to increase feedback for themselves, but that requires teachers to make changes to teaching habits in order to provide the opportunities for learners.

Second, most teachers view curriculum goals and objectives as the content for the teacher to cover. Teachers provide a curriculum goal (and objectives) to students, but not deliberately for explicit interaction (setting objectives and providing feedback), so students have not typically learned to self-evaluate or self-regulate their progress using curriculum objectives, thereby reducing the gaps between what they know and can do and the desired goals for their grade level and subject area.

To change the first issue, an understanding of classroom feedback can be broadened to include tools to deliberately maximize student self-evaluation and peer feedback. A student who knows ways to seek and use feedback other than solely from the teacher responsible for twenty or more students, will become more engaged in the class and achieve better over time. Regarding the second issue, the teacher can deliberately provide curriculum goals and objectives daily, with a strategy and time for students to interact with them.

## PAUSE TO REFLECT

Explain the ways that you and your fellow teachers have deliberately used feedback in a positive way and how you can expand such practices to positively impact student learning.

## FEEDBACK FOR INSTRUCTION, NOT ONLY ASSESSMENT

In the past ten years, meta-analyses have shown that the teacher is the most important school factor to improve student learning (Marzano et al., 2001) and that it is more important to consider the teacher effect rather than the school effect when it comes to improving student achievement (Hattie, 2009). When one stops to think about the amount of time that students spend each day in classrooms, then the impact that teachers have on student learning seems obvious. But, the teacher is not the hinge factor; *the transfer of information* is the hinge factor.

Feedback is typically characterized as assessment of progress toward a goal, but it is also a cue to seek more information or instruction. Think about the typical coversation with your child or another student when you ask, "How are you doing in Class X?" The student responds nonchalantly, "I don't know yet, but I will next week after I take the test." If the student interacts with the curriculum goals at the beginning and throughout the lesson, then the natural process of using feedback to cue an instructional need or opportunity presents itself. It appears that we have missed the opportunity to systematically use feedback in this instructive way.

The best way that a school can provide for a student to learn and use feedback strategies is for the teacher to make teaching changes to incorporate feedback throughout instruction as well as during assessment in every class.

Just as a hinge connects two panels so they can swing relative to each other, feedback is the hinge that swings the information about goals and progress between teacher and student. Teachers who deliberately teach students to use feedback and help-seeking strategies to learn the content of the curriculum objectives report that student engagement increases. As students become more engaged in the learning activities, their actions and self-assessment provide feedback to teachers, who in turn make deliberate decisions to adjust teaching.

Considering feedback as a learning strategy, not just something teachers are required to do, inspires teachers to teach students to self-evaluate and use feedback from others as a critical part of all lessons.

## PAUSE TO REFLECT

What do you think about when you hear the word feedback? Do you think about improvement?

## SMALL CHANGES, POSITIVE GAINS

This book, *Feedback: The Hinge That Joins Teaching and Learning,* is about making small changes in every classroom to dramatically increase student engagement and achievement. This book shares practical examples of how to incorporate instructive feedback into daily lessons by optimizing opportunities for students to seek and receive goal-based feedback through self-regulation and from others, as well as by changing the direction of the feedback so students can learn to initiate feedback productively.

The next chapter, "Positive Deviants," gives a brief but intriguing explanation about a change process that focuses on solutions that are "invisible in plain sight." The change process described there zeroes in on small behaviors within a community that can lead to large gains in an organization, resulting in coveted improvements. The story of the soup and the ladle will inspire some teachers to change their teaching habits slightly. They will find that the solution of changing the direction of feedback in the classroom is as basic as ladling soup differently.

In Chapter 3, "The Tell-Tale Students," I explain the first of various practical feedback tools, a goal accounting template, with examples that require minimal changes to teaching time or materials for any classroom at any age level, from an elementary resource classroom to a high school honors course. A goal accounting template is a student-managed tool that calls attention to the student's progress on curriculum goals and objectives. This powerful student self-regulating technique changes school for underachieving learners. These templates engage every student at the beginning, during, and at the end of every lesson, increasing interaction and achievement. When students use the templates, they provide feedback to teachers about how they perceive their progress; this information has prompted many teachers to find ways to provide better instruction.

Chapter 4, "Learn to Engage," emphasizes strategies that a student can use during a lesson to seek feedback about his or her progress that extend beyond self evaluation to self-teaching, peer interaction or peer teaching, and seeking further instruction from the expert (teacher) in the class. The strategies, turn-and-talk and note taking, are familiar to most teachers and students, but by most accounts, not deliberately used to increase engagement and achievement. Students may have taken notes, for example, as a classroom activity and received points or grades for doing so. As a feedback strategy, students take notes to manage what they know about the curriculum goals and objectives. Because it is written and visible to others, students can use their notes as a tool to seek further information from others. That leads to the other strategy, turn-and-talk, which is a powerful tool to manage feedback orally.

Changing instruction by increasing feedback is significant, but changing assessment adds another opportunity to positively impact student achievement. Criterion-based or standards-based record keeping is a process that increases the teacher-to-student feedback, both as formative and summative assessment. Chapter 5, "Feedback From the Teacher," provides a discussion about the companion technique to the student goal accounting template so that teachers can track and document student performances by goals and objectives during instruction and on assessments.

The final chapter, "Feedback Changed My Teaching," is included for school principals and instructional coaches who work with teachers. This chapter explains how some principals or coaches successfully work side-by-side with teachers to help them incorporate better feedback, instruction, and assessment to learners. The teachers explain the importance of receiving feedback from their colleagues in order to change teaching strategically.

Within each chapter, teachers contribute their personal successes and challenges about making and sustaining changes to instruction based on the hinge factor, feedback. Whether they teach science or English, at the high school or elementary level, in resource or general education classes, teachers have shown that they can incorporate the suggestions because the tools increase student engagement and teach students to become more self-regulated, able to use peer feedback, and motivated to seek feedback from the teacher.

The greatest lesson about the hinge factor, feedback, is that when students become motivated to share their own progress with teachers, the teachers become inspired to teach better.

## PAUSE TO REFLECT

How has your school responded to the need to improve engagement and student achievement?

When observing for feedback in classrooms, which students seem to naturally seek and receive feedback? Could other student behaviors change if the teacher provided a cue or instruction to do so?

# CHAPTER TWO

# POSITIVE DEVIANTS

---

Tena Reese, instructional technology specialist, approached me during a break at a workshop for secondary teachers at her school district in Arkansas. We had been discussing lesson planning when someone asked what I would change in classrooms if I could change "just one thing." Without hesitating, I said that improving feedback would increase student engagement and accelerate student learning.

Tena observed, "I thought I understood feedback until you started talking about it." She explained that when she thought about feedback, she imagined ways teachers give students feedback either verbally in class or written on assignments, which, she said, they already do.

"But, you said that when you observe classes," she continued, "you look for students being given opportunities to seek feedback from the teacher, from their classmates, and in self-reflection. It sounds like you are saying that feedback is something students do. So, now I am confused because I thought feedback was the teacher's job."

The ideas for this book came from discussions in workshops with teachers like Tena. Invariably, I would be addressing an issue about making a change to teaching and someone would offer, "Isn't this what teachers already do?" The answer, of course, is yes, teachers are giving feedback, but when it does not result in the expected gains in student learning, they could change how they use it.

The suggestions in these chapters are slight variations on established teaching habits, so most teachers are willing to make them to be successful.

## PAUSE TO REFLECT

Have you and your colleagues felt that nagging feeling that you are already doing a technique but not seeing student gains as a result?

## THE SOUP AND THE LADLE

When discussing feedback to improve student learning, teachers say they give a lot of feedback, but in his meta-analyses, researcher John Hattie found enough evidence to prompt him to write, "At best, students receive 'moments' of feedback in a single day" (2009, p. 174). The teacher perception and the research findings remind me of the story about the soup and the ladle. In the highlands of Bolivia, a community reported that a small number of children suffered from stunting (short height for their age, as well as neurological impacts). Researchers suggested that it was likely malnutrition, but the elders believed that the soups they made daily were full of protein and vegetables, made the same way by every family in a large kettle over the fire. They did not consider nutrition as the problem since they believed that all community members fed their children well.

When observers watched cooking and serving in the homes, they noticed that in the families whose children did not suffer from stunting, the mothers dipped the ladles deep into the pot in order to give the solid foods to the children and all other members of the family (the positive deviants), whereas in the other families, the children received the broth skimmed off the top of the soup, reserving the solids at the bottom for the workers (Pascale, Sternin, & Sternin, 2010). The community members did make the same nutritious soups, but not all children were fed in the same way. The children who ate the soup skimmed from the top experienced the low-height syndrome. The mothers probably had learned the habit of serving soup by watching and adopting the way their own mothers had done it, and they were not aware of the differences in the ladling. By learning a strategy from the positive deviants in the community, they easily made the change and sustained it over time, resulting in positive gains.

## PAUSE TO REFLECT

Does the soup-and-ladle story translate to any of the teaching and assessing behaviors that you use in your classroom or observe in your school?

## SMALL CHANGES, DRAMATIC RESULTS

"Small" change to organizational behaviors described in the book *The Power of Positive Deviance,* by Richard Pascale, Jerry Sternin, and Monique Sternin (2010), is a different way to improve the results of social issues. The researchers use a change tool that is unusual because it goes against the accepted grain of thinking about how to make dramatic positive increases. They suggest identifying the positive deviants in the organization and replicating their behaviors to increase results. The researchers describe solutions to problems as being "invisible in plain sight" (Pascale et al. 2010, p. 183). A specific observation tactic includes being able to observe carefully to find the hidden behavior "invisible in plain sight" that the positive deviants do that can change results for others. One of the researchers, Larry Sternin, describes the "somersault question," or the "flip," as critical in the process. It takes the topic at hand and literally turns it the other way around (p. 30). In the case of the soup and the ladle, food was not the malnourishment problem; it was the way that the food was being served. That was the behavior that was "invisible in plain sight" and needed to be "flipped."

The authors of the positive deviance tactic focus on solutions that already exist inside the community. They seek even one positive example within a community, so that the recommended change is more easily accepted by everyone. By observing *how* the mothers fed the children, the researchers broke from the conventional wisdom about nutrition. By finding the positive deviants, the authors built on know-how that people already have within the system and figured out ways to remove barriers to enlarge results to match those of the positive deviants.

We have been led to believe that school reform requires big organizational changes. Many valuable tomes on leadership explain how to bring about school reform with system-wide change. For example, in 2010, Michael Fullan's *Motion Leadership: The Skinny on Becoming Change Savvy* notes that bringing about positive change on a large scale is so complex that to do so, getting at the "skinny" is to address the essence, or unobscured issues. The *skinny* refers to the core, unadorned facts, or what you absolutely need to know. Without question, large-scale reform requires particular tools; often the reform also includes changes to the school system for reasons other than student learning gains.

To seek the small solutions—that is, to make gains in student achievement for the small number of disengaged students for whom the conventional tactics of schooling may not be working—one needs to observe classrooms to identify the positive deviants, find the behaviors that are "invisible in plain sight," and teach the others how to make the conceptual "flip."

The soup story gives evidence to the importance of social complexity and observing behaviors, not just listening to what people say about their behaviors and what they believe others are doing as well. Teachers would say that they all give students lots of feedback and that most teachers do it in similar ways. When observing teaching in classrooms, one sees that teachers have strikingly similar habits related to giving feedback. Most teachers give the feedback to students based on activity or task completion, not explicitly tied to curriculum standards and objectives. As we will discuss, changing the feedback loop in the classroom is as simple as changing the way one ladles the soup.

## PAUSE TO REFLECT

Explain how the change tool that Pascale and colleagues refer to as the *power of positive deviance* might work in your school.

## THE FLIP

When observing teaching and learning in classrooms, I began watching the disengaged students. I noticed that they received little to no feedback during classes, even though the teacher had prepared and delivered a good lesson. More successful students (positive deviants) did receive feedback because they appeared to naturally or instinctively initiate feedback for themselves, either by taking the time to reflect, interacting purposefully with peers, or seeking feedback from the teacher. They participated in a few activities that allowed them to be in the fortuitous position to seek and receive help.

The positive deviant behavior was invisible in plain sight: more successful students sought feedback informally, but the less successful students did not. In order to ensure that all of the students could tap into the behavior of seeking feedback, teachers would need to "ladle differently," by recognizing the flip. In this case the flip meant that teachers would not always give the feedback, but instead give opportunities for students to learn to seek feedback for themselves.

To change the direction of feedback and expand the results, teachers could adapt techniques within their existing routines at the beginning, middle, and ends of lessons by providing for ways that students could seek feedback from:

1. *Self:* evaluating or using metacognitive strategies, seeking information or correctives, creating a self-teaching or self-regulating situation

2. *Peers:* clarifying information or processing aloud for confirmation, peer teaching

3. *Teacher:* informal interactions in class, questions designed to seek reteaching, corrections to assignments, test and project evaluations

A pivotal criterion in observing the positive deviant success was that students who knew the focus or topic of the lesson began and remained more engaged than other students because they sought feedback about their own understandings based on the focus or topic of the lesson. Some students came prepared to find out the lesson goal, even when it was not immediately obvious. For that reason, goal setting required teachers to provide the goals (standards and objectives) for the students.

**HINGES IN ACTION**

A good goal(s) is key. The goal is the target for performance; feedback is information about where you stand in relation to the goal and how to improve.

To expand on goal setting, I found that teachers could easily increase feedback to unengaged learners and all learners by providing curriculum goals for the learners at the beginning of every lesson and returning to those goals at the end of the lesson. For many teachers, this meant a change from writing an agenda on the board, to providing curriculum standards and objectives. The students need directions about how to interact with the goals and time to do so. For many teachers, setting an objective at the beginning of the class is not new, but the notion that the students interact with the goal is new. A practical way to do so is described in detail in the next chapter: using goal accounting templates. These templates are tools that students use to interact with the curriculum goals and objectives, allowing them to self-evaluate, monitor, and regulate throughout a lesson and unit. At various times, a student might share his evaluation with peers or the teacher, improving the chances of receiving feedback that is informal, yet formative, creating an environment for more instruction or information.

**PAUSE TO REFLECT**

Does the idea of asking students to interact with a goal, verbally or by writing it down, present a new way of goal setting for you as a teacher or for the teachers in your building?

## MAKING THE SMALL CHANGES

Feedback, as described in the previous chapter, can be characterized as assessment of progress toward a goal, but also as a cue to seek more information or instruction. The coming chapters provide the research and show how other high-yield strategies such as note taking and cooperative learning maximize feedback opportunities within lessons, resulting in better student engagement throughout a lesson. The disengaged student can use traditional strategies to seek feedback from self, peers, and the teacher in order to be more involved in his or her own learning.

Teachers acknowledge that students who do not take notes well, or give up on the process during class, perform less proficiently than those who take notes effortlessly. Students who do not pair and share with their partners during times designated to do so do not do as well as those who take advantage of time to process aloud. Students who ask questions to initiate feedback both on their own understandings and to seek more information about a topic stay motivated to learn. Those who do not remain disengaged.

In fact, some teachers tell me that what they observe about their own behavior is that when students do not use techniques readily right away, the teacher drops the technique in favor of giving directions, or as teachers say, "doing it for them [students]." Identifying to students and teachers the three strategies that will make them more aware of the power of feedback increases the possibility of advancing on curriculum goals.

In addition to instructional feedback, formative assessment and summative assessment feedback becomes more powerful to the learner when those data are deliberately organized by standards and objectives. Chapter 5 discusses that type of strategy. As a companion to the goal accounting templates that students learn to use, some teachers begin to track student performance during the class period and share the results with students. Teachers find that becoming more aware of student performance during class increases the possibility of differentiating instruction and simply changing lesson plans to more accurately provide instruction that is appropriate for a group of students. The teachers use a low-tech clipboard and class roster, but it works. Also discussed in Chapter 5 is how teachers use electronic scoring of assignments and assessments to the standards and objectives, or criterion-based scoring, to provide more descriptive evaluative information or feedback.

Teachers in schools know what works for students, because in every class there are students who perform well. Using the positive deviant theory, we ask teachers to identify students who do well and which techniques those students use consistently, in class, to perform and progress toward proficiency of the curriculum goals, *even when it is hard to do, or means that the teacher has to change teaching habits.* We can also use the positive deviant change tool to identify situations in some schools in which students make gains as a result of teachers becoming more aware of feedback, and replicating those practices in other classrooms.

## PAUSE TO REFLECT

How can students and teachers be positive deviants in your school?

# CHAPTER THREE

# THE TELL-TALE STUDENTS

---

In *The Tell-Tale Brain,* V. S. Ramachandran (2011) draws medical attention away from organs such as the spleen to the tell-tale brain in order to explain what makes us work. A tell-tale is an indicator that gives warning about something. In *Moby Dick,* the compass on the ceiling in the captain's quarters is the tell-tale because it gives the captain information he needs to change the ship's direction. The brain is the tell-tale of the human being, Ramachandran believes. The brain sends out the indicators and the warnings for movement and the workings of the mind. Once dubbed the "Marco Polo of neuroscience" by Richard Dawkins, Ramachandran explains that humans are the most exciting upheaval on the great Darwinian stage since the creation of life itself and that brain science "has advanced at an astonishing pace over the last fifteen years lending fresh perspectives on, well, just about everything. After decades of floundering in the shadow of the hard sciences, the age of neuroscience has truly dawned" (p. xii).

Ramachandran is well known for his work on phantom limbs, the neuroscientific explanation for why amputees still feel their limbs, as well as how to relieve the pain or itching when their appendages are no longer there. Ramachandran writes that he used mirrors and a cardboard box to figure it out. He appreciates the fancy brain imaging equipment, but claims that he has been very successful by listening, watching, and hypothesizing. His method, he insists, is the scientific method; his tools are very basic. The researcher writes unapologetically about combining the scientific method with simple, not fancy, techniques.

## TELL-TALE STUDENTS

Teachers and principals should also trust their instincts when they see tell-tale students disengage, and the educators also should be unapologetic about using simple methodology to find solutions. In a classroom, the tell-tale students who disengage during the lesson indicate to us at that moment that our teaching technique is not helping them learn well. We can see it as an opportunity to change direction. This chapter shows teachers ways to help students focus on the curriculum goals (the standards and objectives) for each lesson. Goal setting prepares students for lessons in which they can use powerful help-seeking strategies (e.g., from self, peers, and the teacher) without waiting for broad-scale initiatives to provide expensive equipment and software. The school equivalent of mirrors and a cardboard box—the goal accounting templates (GATs)—spur learning and can easily be adapted to most classes.

The first step to increasing feedback opportunities in class-room instruction is providing goals (standards and objectives) of the lesson, because that sets the topic that can be taught and assessed in that time frame.

**PAUSE TO REFLECT**

Does it help to think of disengaged students as the tell-tales for instruction? Do they give warnings to the teacher to adjust the strategies for processing and learning the information?

## FEEDBACK AND GOAL SETTING

Feedback is tied to goal setting. As mentioned in Chapter 1, setting objectives and providing feedback show a large effect size ($d = 0.61$), considered to be very powerful to increase student achievement. While not a new concept, learning techniques to set personal goals can be extremely powerful to advance one's knowledge or skills. It appears that the reason it works is because in addition to providing a focus for a person's attention and efforts, it also increases confidence and promotes persistence over time. While just about anyone you know can make a New Year's resolution, for example, your friends who set attainable goals and track progress are motivated to stay the course. In addition, feedback from others, both peers and experts, helps your friend improve the chances of success by adjusting, adapting, and seeking information.

As teachers, we have the opportunity at the beginning of every class period to teach students to interact with a curriculum goal (engage), to use class time to teach information about the content using correctives and clarifications from the teacher, peers, and self (feedback), and teach self-regulation techniques so students learn to advance (achieve) on the curriculum goals. What connects engagement to feedback to achievement is goal setting.

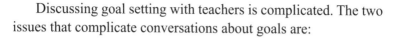

Discussing goal setting with teachers is complicated. The two issues that complicate conversations about goals are:

1. Teachers do write the curriculum standards on the board or on lesson plans but do not ask students to interact with the goal as a performance goal or motivator.

2. Students do not expect to self-regulate or self-assess on a regular basis since teachers generally grade and report their progress.

### HINGES IN ACTION

Interacting with the goal(s) produces positive results. When you determine where you stand in relation to a goal(s), you become motivated to seek help or information. In class, a student has the opportunity to receive feedback from the teacher, but also can learn to self-regulate.

Let's return to feedback as the hinge factor that creates a productive tension between student and teacher that intentionally improves learning new information, but also increases engagement. In every class, a teacher can judiciously provide the goal (standard and objective) and the opportunity for the student to interact with it. Some teachers may ask students to say the goal out loud in chorus, write it down, or give a thumbs-up or down, to show their understanding about the content of the goal. During each class period, students can use feedback from the teacher, peers, and self to increase the likelihood of reducing the gap between what he or she knows about a topic or skill and what is possible, only if the student becomes aware of the goal. The next section describes how teachers and students use a goal accounting template in every class as a way to become more deliberate about interacting with the goals (standards and objectives).

## PAUSE TO REFLECT

How do teachers set the goal in your school(s)? Do students learn to interact with the curriculum goals during each lesson?

## FEEDBACK: SELF

High school history teacher Trevor Collins created a goal accounting template, the "Student Effort and Understanding Self-Assessment," that students use every day in class to self-score on lesson objectives (see Figure 3.1).

Trevor teaches at a K–12 school near Knoxville, Tennessee, where traditions run deep. In fact, most of Trevor's teachers remember him as a student. Given those conditions of social complexity, one would assume that it would be difficult for a teacher to change any practices, first because of his own "automatic teaching," but also because the cultural resistance might press firmly against change.

At first, Trevor acknowledged that he thought he used district standards by posting them on a bulletin board, but had not considered the standards as guidance for students for their daily work. With sincerity, he said that he posted them because it was the school policy to do so. Now Trevor begins every lesson by projecting the goals for the lesson on the board (derived from state standards and objectives). For example:

Know about progressivism in the early 1900s in the United States

Presidents: Roosevelt versus Wilson

**Figure 3.1** Trevor Collins Goal Accounting Template (GAT)

| | Student Effort and Understanding Self-Assessment | | | | |
|---|---|---|---|---|---|

**United States History Objectives**

Unit: _____

Name: _____ Period: _____

Project for Unit: _____

| Date | Text Section | Objective / Goal for the Day | Effort Rating (0–5) | Understanding Before Lesson (0–5) | After Lesson (0–5) |
|---|---|---|---|---|---|
| | | | Pre:<br>Post: | | |
| | | | Pre:<br>Post: | | |
| | | | Pre:<br>Post: | | |
| | | | Pre:<br>Post: | | |
| | | | Pre:<br>Post: | | |
| | | | Pre:<br>Post: | | |
| | | | Pre:<br>Post: | | |
| | | | Pre:<br>Post: | | |
| | | | Pre:<br>Post: | | |
| | | | Pre:<br>Post: | | |
| | | | Pre:<br>Post: | | |
| | | | Pre:<br>Post: | | |
| | | | Pre:<br>Post: | | |

*Source: Improving Student Learning One Teacher at a Time*, (p. 118), by Jane Pollock. Alexandria, VA: ASCD. © 2007 by ASCD. Reprinted and adapted with permission. Learn more about ASCD at www.ascd.org.

Students complete the top part of the self-scoring document, and then daily fill in the date, text section, and objectives that the teacher provides. Trevor asks the students to score themselves on the topic understandings before and at the end of class, as well as scoring themselves on their effort when the class begins and at the end of class. The template is glued into their notebooks so students can be ready to turn to the section to take notes as soon as they complete the form.

The next day, the students write the same goal about progressivism, but the specific objective is related to corporations and monopolies (not the roles of the presidents). The third day, they address the social work and child labor. Each day, as the students write the objectives and score themselves on their understandings and effort, they realize that the three days (and all of the assignments) related to their understanding the Progressive Era, so they can see their own progress.

Trevor provides a simple scoring rubric for the students to use to self-assess (see Figure 3.2).

**Figure 3.2**   Trevor Collins Scoring Rubric

|   | Effort Rubric |   | Understanding Rubric |
|---|---|---|---|
| 5 | I work until I complete and push myself to exceed the minimum work required. | 5 | I could teach the class! |
| 4 | I work until it is complete. | 4 | I can talk about it with classmates. |
| 3 | I give it some effort and ask questions to clarify my understanding. | 3 | I know it but have questions. |
| 2 | I give it some effort, but stop when it becomes tough. | 2 | I somewhat understand it. |
| 1 | I give it very little effort. | 1 | I have no idea! |

Regarding student self-assessment, researcher Marzano writes, "Having students track their [own] progress using [a] rubric is a hidden gem. This strategy involves multiple types of assessments, increases interactions between teachers and students, and provides students with clear guidance on how to enhance their learning" (2009, p. 87).

Trevor writes about the change in student engagement in an e-mail he sent:

I can remember being told, during my student teaching as an undergraduate, to always write a standard and objective as the first component of a lesson plan. I also remember that the form we were presented with was lengthy and required a large amount of time to complete. Although I continued to use curriculum standards in my daily lessons, I didn't fully understand the importance of recognizing them as learning goals for student performance. I never really thought of it as a tool for the students to use; it was a tool to guide my instruction from a teacher's point of view. I also was prepared to put it on the board because it was what the principal asked us to do. I am pretty sure that it was related to what I taught, but did not truly guide my teaching each day.

So, I wrote an objective on my dry erase board for years; however, now I realize that allowing the students to see the standard is not enough. The students need to understand what is being presented to them and why it is important. Using a goal accounting template has made my students more aware of what is being asked of them both because it is an assessment, but it also cues them to ask for more information or re-teaching. The template also allows me to look at each individual student's achievement. I can, within a few minutes of monitoring my student's notebooks, get a clear picture of the level of understanding from the student point of view.

I'm not excited to admit that I have, in the past, taught a lesson and trudged along without a lot of regard to student understanding. Now I can look at the students' own personal scores, on a scale of 1 to 5, and get a firm grasp of what they know. It only takes a couple of weeks before they begin to realize that their understanding and effort ratings have a direct tie to their achievement on classroom assignments, quizzes, tests. When the students begin to realize that "luck" doesn't have anything to do with grades in class, they tend to realize they need to put more effort toward learning the content.

Ironically, knowing how they evaluate themselves has made me put more effort into teaching to their needs and not just cover the history curriculum.

This is an example of the soup and the ladle. Trevor tells me that he is a teacher who has the same resources as any other teacher (the soup), but ladles it differently now in order to increase student engagement. When I observed Trevor's classes, the beginning of the lesson was inviting, fluid, and academic. As the high school students entered and briefly greeted each other and the teacher, they took out spiral notebooks without any prompting and started writing the objective that Trevor had projected, giving themselves scores. Every student participated. I asked one student if he minded filling out the sheets and he responded that no, he wished all of his teachers would ask them to use the goal sheets so he could follow along better in every class.

Watching Trevor walk among the students peering over their shoulders as he lectured, I noticed that sometimes they commented to him or pointed to their notebooks. Because they had a structure for interacting with the daily objectives, all students became more focused at the beginning of the lesson and this carried over throughout the lesson. Near the end of the class period, Trevor stopped a few minutes before the bell rang and asked the students to reassess.

The students self-assessed, but they also gave Trevor feedback by the scores they wrote for themselves. During the final few minutes of the class, Trevor could once again walk around the classroom glancing at the students' score sheets to see how they evaluated their understandings and effort as a result of the instruction.

When the students later received assignments or test scores, they could see the patterns of their classroom scores and how well their judgments of effort and understandings prepared them for assessments.

At the end of the school year, Trevor wrote again:

On a celebration note, I received my End of Course Test results yesterday. Out of the students that tested, 14 scored proficient. Proficient is the score the state wants all students to be at for the course. The remaining students all scored in the Advanced category.

These are the highest raw scores that I have ever had. Thanks for the guidance throughout this year. I believe the summer will be a time of reflection.

## PAUSE TO REFLECT

Trevor Collins uses a goal accounting template to provide the standards and objectives to students each class. How would you adapt the goal templates for your grade level and subject area?

Using a modified version of the goal accounting template, Teresa Langum provides key words or text to aid the students as they write their objectives (see Figure 3.3).

## PAUSE TO REFLECT

Many teachers modify the goal accounting templates for special populations; how would you change the forms to meet student needs?

Teresa indicates that she simply does it to save time, but she could also use the partially prepared templates to differentiate for some students. Since Teresa teaches middle school, she indicates that the goals create a strong transition from one subject to the next by helping students focus specifically on the academic vocabulary and the personal connection to the content.

## FEEDBACK: EFFORT

Jenny Humble's templates are modified for an elementary class. Realizing the importance of having students interact with the goal, she created a template so that students could track not only their effort and understanding, but also their homework assignments related to the goals (see Figure 3.4).

Because Jenny's students score themselves in various subjects throughout the day (reading, math, writing, science, social studies), she streamlined the document and added the scoring scale. Some of her students like to use different colored pens to score themselves at the beginning and end of the lesson, emphasizing how their understanding increased.

**Figure 3.3**   Teresa Langum Goal Accounting Template

Name _____ Date _____ Hour _____

Chapter name _____ Lesson _____

Overall personal goal for this unit _____

Plan for achieving this goal _____

| Date | Pages | Objective/Goal for the Day | Effort Rating (0-5) | Understanding Rating (0-5) |
|---|---|---|---|---|
| 3/28/2011 Mon. | 296–305 | Explain results/_____ of Henry Ford's assembly _____. | before     after | before     after |
| 3/29/2011 Tues. | 296–308 | Explain results/effects of Henry _____'s assembly line. | | |
| 3/30/2011 Wed. | none | Demonstrate and evaluate _____ 1. Assemble by yourself 2. Assemble using assembly line | | |
| 3/31/2011 Thurs. | 310–316 | Identify _____ changes of the _____'s with web notes. | | |
| 4/1/2011 Fri. | none | Open _____ Benchmark practice debriefing. | | |
| 4/4/2011 Mon. | 310–316 | Summarize _____ changes of the _____'s with web notes. | | |
| 4/5/2011 Tues. | 320–327 | Identify causes and _____ of the Great _____ w/ C/E chart. | | |
| 4/6/2011 Wed. | none | Open response Benchmark practice. | | |

*Source: Improving Student Learning One Teacher at a Time,* (p. 118), by Jane Pollock. Alexandria, VA: ASCD. © 2007 by ASCD. Reprinted and adapted with permission. Learn more about ASCD at www .ascd.org.

**Figure 3.4** Jenny Humble Reading Student Effort and Understanding Self-Assessment

| | Student Effort and Understanding Self-Assessment | | | | |
|---|---|---|---|---|---|
| | Date | Objective for the Day | Effort | Understand | HW |
| Reading | | | 0 1 2 3 4 | 0 1 2 3 4 | |
| | | | 0 1 2 3 4 | 0 1 2 3 4 | |
| | | | 0 1 2 3 4 | 0 1 2 3 4 | |
| | | | 0 1 2 3 4 | 0 1 2 3 4 | |
| | | | 0 1 2 3 4 | 0 1 2 3 4 | |
| | | | 0 1 2 3 4 | 0 1 2 3 4 | |
| | | | 0 1 2 3 4 | 0 1 2 3 4 | |
| | | | 0 1 2 3 4 | 0 1 2 3 4 | |
| | | | 0 1 2 3 4 | 0 1 2 3 4 | |
| | | | 0 1 2 3 4 | 0 1 2 3 4 | |
| | | | 0 1 2 3 4 | 0 1 2 3 4 | |
| | | | 0 1 2 3 4 | 0 1 2 3 4 | |
| | | | 0 1 2 3 4 | 0 1 2 3 4 | |
| | | | 0 1 2 3 4 | 0 1 2 3 4 | |
| | | | 0 1 2 3 4 | 0 1 2 3 4 | |
| | | | 0 1 2 3 4 | 0 1 2 3 4 | |
| | | | 0 1 2 3 4 | 0 1 2 3 4 | |
| | | | 0 1 2 3 4 | 0 1 2 3 4 | |
| | | | 0 1 2 3 4 | 0 1 2 3 4 | |

Jenny wrote about the score sheets to describe them to other teachers interested in using them at the elementary level:

> The goal sheets provide great feedback to students about how effort relates to understanding. Fifth graders know what effort is, but they don't know how effort affects their understanding. From the feedback, my students saw not only how their effort affected a particular assignment, but also how long-term effort affected their understanding over an entire unit.
>
> As a class, we frequently discussed how effort affected their understanding, and students shared in groups using their goal sheet as evidence to show how effort and understanding were related. Students commented how "putting in effort," meant "my grades go up," and that "just listening isn't okay."
>
> After using the goal sheets and discussing the feedback the students gleaned from it, student achievement increased in all subject areas. Also, student engagement increased. When students weren't talking in a group, I didn't point out their participation, I pointed out their effort. Participation is evident in a group, but when I give feedback about effort, that is something that is seen in all subjects at all times. Providing feedback from the scoring sheet placed a priority on effort when engaging in all aspects of the class, such as listening, viewing, and speaking, which then improved their understanding no matter the concept.

When Jenny discussed her templates with other teachers in her district, she stressed that she became motivated to provide better feedback to her students because she became increasingly aware of how responsive they were to changing their effort when they knew how well they did or could perform on the standards and objectives. She described one of her students, who we will call Katrina, who had always required a few extra directions or behavioral comments until she started to use the goal sheet. When Katrina began to self-evaluate and write it down so she could see it over a week, she began to respond to feedback about making an effort: following along in read-aloud text, answering questions in class, or talking during partner interaction. Jenny said:

> I could physically see her body language shift during lessons as she self-monitored her effort. Because of the feedback about effort, students like Katrina learned to self-evaluate or self-assess, and that's a lifelong skill they'll use in everything they do. I knew my objective of teaching effort-understanding relationship was effective when students began conversations with me about their objective sheets. They didn't simply fill out the template; they wanted to see the feedback that indicated how their effort paid off, and they wanted to show it off to me.

## PAUSE TO REFLECT

Jenny Humble noticed that she became more interested in student performances as they evaluated themselves. Would you have similar opportunities to view student evaluations during class?

## FEEDBACK FROM PEERS
## AND FEEDBACK TO THE TEACHER

Middle school English teacher Katie DeBoer describes one of the key ways that student engagement increased in her class was when the students used the goal templates with a "turn-and-talk" strategy. Just as other teachers indicate the important focus on the goal and the transition from one subject to the next, Katie noticed that when she directed students to talk to their table partners about their understandings before and at the end of the class, students were more likely to seek feedback and clarification from each other, and much more likely to ask her questions in order to extend their learning.

Because the students were comfortable scoring themselves and sharing their evaluations with each other, she also noticed students were eager to ask each other to see the goal templates from each other from days when they might have been absent. Students were much more likely to ask about previous activities because the goal templates provided an opportunity and a cue to do so.

Katie reflected on her student performances:

> As an educator I have always believed that I interacted well and built great relationships with my students, but I frequently wondered if our interaction was purposeful. The goal accounting templates have provided a way for my students and me to have rich dialogue about their learner goals and set a purpose as their learning endeavors continue.
>
> Prior to using the goal accounting templates, I never actually knew how well my students had learned until after I assessed each student's work. I would collect assignments, give comments on the assignments, and then pass the assignments back. Sounds familiar, doesn't it? I often wondered how many students grew as learners based on my comments and realized that often I was late in getting papers back so we were already working on a new goal in some cases before they had feedback on the previous assignments.
>
> I knew I had to change how I was providing feedback to the learners because I was spending a lot of time grading and all of a sudden it was obvious to me that my time was not productive. Creating goal forms took some time on my part, but during this process it made me reevaluate what I was teaching. If I couldn't develop a learner goal for an application the students would complete, I was able to give myself

immediate feedback—what was the purpose of my students completing that application of their learning?

Goal accounting templates provide me with a way to see if a student is not only meeting and understanding the learner goal, but also provides me with a student's personal reflection: what did they learn/accomplish by completing the goal and a question they still have regarding the goal. There are five columns on my score sheets: the learner goal, the student's effort, the student's understanding, a quick reflection about what they learned or accomplished, and questions they still have.

The templates help me differentiate learning in my classroom and provide the learner with immediate feedback and motivate me to instruct students one on one. The goal sheets are used to group students based on questions, for example, if a group of students still have a question on incorporating imagery into their writing after a mini lesson has already been taught, I can provide direct instruction to that specific group of individuals before they move on to the next learner goal.

Finally, using goal accounting templates every day provides a purpose for student and teacher interaction, lets students know how to improve or continue their learning, and informs the teacher *while* students are learning, *not after.*

## PAUSE TO REFLECT

Does Katie's experience resonate with your experiences with providing feedback to learners?

## FEEDBACK THROUGHOUT THE CLASS

Danielle Stevens, a high school business teacher, commented on how much she likes the way that the students become more involved in the class because she can ask them to return to the goal various times, which she said works well when the class periods are longer or double periods. She said that before she used the goal accounting templates, she would ask the class as a whole whether they understood, and if the majority of the students responded positively, she moved on. Danielle muses that as a volleyball coach, she realizes the power of individual assessment and feedback, so she has incorporated the goal forms into her class so that students repeatedly evaluate their performances during class now so that the instruction becomes more specifically directed at the students' needs.

In addition, Danielle added the language objectives to her templates as a way to address the needs of the English language learners (see Figure 3.5).

## PAUSE TO REFLECT

Danielle modifies the goal accounting templates for English language learners. Can you think of other ways to adapt the goal accounting templates?

## FEEDBACK IN AN INSTANT

Not too long ago at dinner, I noticed my son, Sam, surreptitiously texting—again. There we were in the middle of a family gathering, platters clacking as they were passed around, requests for salt and pepper shouted above the normal conversation, laughter. And there he was, furtively texting. Later that evening, I mentioned to him that I noticed he was texting, but before I could firmly advise him about table manners, he looked at me, surprised. Then, he smiled, took out his iPhone, and showed me a graph. "Mom, I was entering my calories—want to see my charts for the week? I have an application, an app. It shows my caloric intake and my workout times, both in numeric values as well as in graph form.

**Figure 3.5** Danielle Stevens Business Goal Accounting Template

## Travel and Tourism Objectives and Comprehension Self-Assessment

| Date | Standard | Content Objectives | Language Objectives | Effort (0–5) | Comprehension (0–5) |
|------|----------|-------------------|---------------------|--------------|---------------------|
|      |          |                   |                     |              |                     |
|      |          |                   |                     |              |                     |
|      |          |                   |                     |              |                     |
|      |          |                   |                     |              |                     |
|      |          |                   |                     |              |                     |
|      |          |                   |                     |              |                     |
|      |          |                   |                     |              |                     |
|      |          |                   |                     |              |                     |
|      |          |                   |                     |              |                     |

Name _____     Class Period _____

*Source: Improving Student Learning One Teacher at a Time,* (p. 118), by Jane Pollock. Alexandria, VA: ASCD. © 2007 by ASCD. Reprinted and adapted with permission. Learn more about ASCD at www.ascd.org.

It calculates for me how many calories I need to either consume or burn off. Then, I e-mail it to myself and I can look at various graphs to note the patterns over a period of time. It helps me figure out what I need to do to stay in shape for hockey."

It is the twenty-first century and no doubt, Sam shares those data with his coaches, his peers, and anyone else who can provide useful feedback or more information to him to meet his personal best. I thought, if my son could use a "calorie app," why couldn't students have a "scoring app" to track their progress on assignments in school so they could track or plot their own progress toward personal-best academic achievement?

Although the goal accounting templates are low tech, they do provide a paper scoring app for students to become aware of and track their own performances so they purposefully seek help from the teacher and their peers. Using online software applications, students and teachers can create electronic versions of the goal accounting template.

## PAUSE TO REFLECT

How do students ask and receive feedback in their athletic or extra-curricular activities?

## FEEDBACK WORKS TO ENGAGE

To recap, teachers who adapt and use the goal accounting templates to teach students to evaluate their own understandings and effort related to the curriculum standards for every lesson are surprised by how quickly students change their interaction in class. When the students interact deliberately with the goal, they self-assess and at once become more focused and engaged in the learning process. Teachers report that the goal sheets work because using them creates a structure for the beginning and end of every lesson; the routine encourages students to begin and end the class by having an opportunity to self-assess and receive feedback from peers and the teacher.

The goal accounting templates are a great example of formative assessment, observed Jenny. She said that the written goals motivated her to walk around the classroom to see how the children score themselves because that gave her feedback from the student perspective. As she moved around the room, she was more likely to interact with students because they asked or because their evaluations gave her the cues she needed to provide instructional comments. Teachers who walk around looking at the scores begin to track the data on simple charts to document the formative assessment, as we will see in a subsequent chapter.

One issue, Jenny said, is that some teachers have curriculum documents that lend themselves to efficient portability to the score sheets, but others do not. In order to make the goal accounting templates manageable, it helps to have a good curriculum document.

## A GOOD SET OF GOALS

Setting goals at the beginning of a lesson is not new to teachers, but having students interact with the goals is new. Fortunately, each state has produced curriculum goals or standards, and they are available online. The curriculum standards in math, history, art, or any other subject can be adapted for a specific grade level and unpacked so that the broad statements clearly indicate the daily instructional objectives.

When teachers use and unpack curriculum standards, such as the new Common Core Standards (articulated by grade levels or courses), as the aim for student performance, they stop perceiving the standards as a checklist for their teaching and begin to revise them specifically so that students can use them for self-assessment. Teachers become aware of the fact that most students become more engaged in class with frequent and purposeful feedback to students about their progress toward the daily goals, including strategically providing ample opportunities for students to receive feedback from peers and self.

These statements reflect many teachers' current practices:

1. Teachers post objectives as compliance rather than providing them to students to provide a marker for feedback throughout instruction and assessment.

   - Teachers do not typically use standards and objectives to guide lesson planning; they write state or district standards on their lesson plan to show that they are doing their jobs.
   - Teachers' lessons indicate that they perceive objectives for the "teaching" part of the lesson and not for learners to use deliberately in self-assessment.

2. When standards and objectives are written in "kid language," they usually result in activities as opposed to goals and objectives.

   - Activity goals are sometimes qualified as being "higher on Bloom's taxonomy," although lessons show scant evidence that students perform at higher levels of cognition.

The "standards-based" goals and objectives, since the original set of math standards in 1989 by the National Council of Teachers of Mathematics (NCTM), are written to show what students should know and be able to do. Using current state or Common Core standards documents that are readily available online, a teacher will see statements such as this variation of subjects in the California standards:

- *[Students] know* the states of matter (solid, liquid, gas) depend on molecular motion.
- *[Students] know* proper food handling safety when preparing meals and snacks.
- *[Students] understand* that a two-dimensional figure is congruent to another if the second can be obtained from the first by a sequence of rotations, reflections, and translations.
- *[Students] can* cite several pieces of textual evidence to support analysis of what the text says explicitly, as well as inferences drawn from the text.

For every subject area, standards can be unpacked to the specificity of daily objectives so that teachers can create a multitude of different activities to instruct students to *get better* at the standards.

In a first grade literacy example, teacher Jenny Felts unpacked a standard:

L.1.5 With guidance and support from adults, demonstrate understanding of word relationships and nuances in word meanings.

    a. Sort words into categories (e.g., colors, clothing) to gain a sense of the concepts the categories represent.

    b. Define word by category and by one or more key attributes (e.g. a duck is a bird that swims; a tiger is a large cat with stripes).

In this example, Jenny would teach the students to sort and describe words by attributes. The students can respond clearly to "I can sort words into categories." After various assignments, the data collected to the unpacked standards give her ample evidence that the student(s) "demonstrate understanding of word relationships and nuances in meanings."

The standards, unpacked, are for students to know the aim of the lesson or series of lessons. The curriculum guide full of materials and mapping according to the standards is the teacher resource to guide the development and delivery of instruction and assessment.

## PAUSE TO REFLECT

After seeing how other teachers unpacked the standards, how do you think that teachers in your school would use your curriculum documents?

## INVISIBLE IN PLAIN SIGHT

In the previous chapter, researchers discussed a tool in research that can produce unusually productive results with minor changes. Pascale, Sternin, and Sternin share improvements from nutrition and health in Somalia to agricultural improvements in Vietnam, and they describe the solution in every case as "invisible in plain sight" (2010, p. 183). They believe that the know-how to improve already exists and by finding the positive deviants all one has to do is figure out ways to remove barriers to enlarge results to match those of the positive deviants.

The goals that all learners, and specifically the tell-tale students, need are "invisible in plain sight" in classrooms; they are the standards and objectives that can be used daily as student goals. In the previous chapter, we discussed the types of feedback that students could initiate or conduct themselves in order to improve performances on the goals:

1. *Self:* evaluating or using metacognitive strategies, seeking information or correctives, creating a self-teaching situation

2. *Peer:* clarifying information or processing aloud for confirmation, peer teaching

3. *Teacher:* informal interactions in class, questions designed to seek reteaching, corrections to assignments, test and project evaluations

Many teachers find that by adapting a set of standards documents, they can modify the goal accounting templates to fit student needs. Once tell-tale students have the goals, they engage more readily throughout the class, seeking help from the teacher, self, peers, and by indirect feedback. As they complete their templates, the students become more adept and accurate at evaluating their own understandings and needs, becoming independent and successful learners.

## PAUSE TO REFLECT

What kinds of challenges would your students experience using a goal accounting template? How could you adapt it for them?

Explain feedback as a hinge factor and how engagement changes for tell-tale students who begin to employ a specific self-regulating technique such as the goal accounting template.

# CHAPTER FOUR

# LEARN TO ENGAGE

A postbehaviorist view of feedback, information processing theory, introduces an expectation that errors are an important part of learning (Locke & Latham, 2002). Researchers Kulhavy and Stock (1989) describe verification and elaboration as two factors that learners employ in order to use feedback in an informational and productive manner. Verification is the simple task of determining whether the answer is correct or incorrect. Elaboration is the informational process that guides a learner in the direction of correct answers. Classroom instruction can provide the learner the opportunity for elaboration, not just error correction, when teachers provide time and a technique to do so. Teachers intuitively know that frequent and relevant feedback increases student engagement, error correction, and other positive consequences; however, they need to perceive managing feedback as viable and manageable in a classroom of twenty to thirty students.

In the previous chapter, students learned to use goal accounting templates, or GATs, primarily for self-regulation in each lesson and throughout a unit. In this chapter, educators discuss ways to teach students to identify errors and become more aware of misconceptions by seeking feedback and instructional support from others in the class. The types of feedback students can use in a class may include:

1. *Self:* evaluating or using metacognitive strategies, seeking information or correctives, creating a self-teaching situation
2. *Peer:* clarifying information or processing aloud for confirmation, peer teaching
3. *Teacher:* informal interactions in class, questions designed to seek reteaching, corrections to assignments, test and project evaluation

When I was observing classrooms for feedback opportunities, one principal told me that it was like looking into the dark with night-vision equipment for the first time. We noted that teachers used familiar high-yield strategies, but the teachers did not use them to deliberately engage all students. In the next section, teachers discuss how to motivate the unmotivated by using the familiar strategies of turn-and-talk and taking notes to manage and maximize feedback to students.

## WAS I *THAT* TEACHER?

Ian Mulligan teaches physics, biology, and elective courses in science, as well as coaching soccer. As part of his coursework for a master's degree in educational leadership, Ian asked me to observe and give him feedback about his teaching. In an essay for his class, he wrote about the observation:

> During the first visit, I thought that my colleague [the author, Jane E. Pollock] would be watching how I teach, like the supervisors did in student teaching. I was surprised that she walked around the room looking over students' shoulders as they took notes, or didn't. Honestly, I wondered why she

wasn't looking at me. When we debriefed, she was complimentary about my delivery and classroom management, but I was surprised when she asked about the three or four students who put their heads down or were not taking notes.

How was I supposed to teach those students who did not want to be engaged?

At first, Ian seemed uneasy that the comments were focused on the students, especially the students he identified as "not wanting to be there, but needing the credit." He was more accustomed to having observers complete a checklist of strategies, commenting about how well he differentiated, infused technology, or addressed difficult content. He had planned a good lesson, delivered the material well, but missed the chance to engage the "tell-tale" four or five students as a result of the instruction.

As he thought about the past few years of teaching, he shared with me:

If anyone came in and saw my classroom in my first few years of teaching, they wouldn't have left with any doubt that the classroom experience was a product of my own learning experience. My slide presentations were well organized and easy to follow. The labs provided more "hands-on" learning following the book. The primary feedback a student received in my class was a test or quiz score from me after a few days of instruction. This type of classroom model was easy for me to maintain classroom control and produce a grade for each student; they were expected to keep up.

I read lines on a slide and explain them in further detail, assuming that every student anxiously awaited my next word. *Was I really that teacher?*

I remembered being bored and disengaged in class as a student, and here I was offering that same experience to my students. Were my students as disengaged as I sometimes felt in class? I was certain that they were struggling to stay focused and keep up each day of class, and more importantly, were not really learning the content.

Ian became motivated to change student engagement, if there were really a solution that would work with high school students. He said that he had spent a lot of time preparing lessons and assessments, but had not really had an opportunity to learn techniques to keep the class dynamic. He made it his goal to address disengagement before, and as it happened:

> Glazed looks, heads down, staring out the window, and even being quiet or not disruptive became feedback to me that students were disengaging—it turned into an exciting challenge. My years of soccer coaching clicked: I cannot run for the players. To have more stamina in a game, the players have to do the running.
>
> As a "science guy," I began to realize how badly students needed me to teach them to use tools to engage themselves in their own learning, even when they did not want to. To be more engaged in class, students have to learn methods and practice them every day.

## PAUSE TO REFLECT

How does Ian Mulligan's soccer coaching realization help him understand students' need for feedback in a class?

### SIMPLE TECHNIQUE: TURN-AND-TALK

Ian's tell-tale or disengaged students motivated him to increase feedback, the hinge factor, to raise engagement and achievement. He introduced the goal accounting templates for the beginning and ends of lessons to encourage self-regulation, but noted that a ninety-minute block was a long time and easy for students to disengage.

Because Ian recognized that large class size limited his ability as a teacher to provide frequent error correction and elaboration for individual needs, he focused on strategies for students to seek and give feedback to peers frequently and purposefully during lectures. He said the following:

> I occasionally used a turn-and-talk in my classroom, but I didn't recognize it as an opportunity for increasing student-to-student feedback so they did not have to wait for me, the teacher, to give them feedback. In fact, I'm not really sure why I used it other than to give myself a few minutes to arrange my presentation or address an unexpected interruption. I had not strategically timed or tied the partner-sharing to information processing for clarification, correction, or generating new ideas.

As mentioned in Chapter 1, *Classroom Instruction That Works* (Marzano et al., 2001) recommends that teachers use high-yield instructional strategies that exceed 0.5 standard deviations (p. 7). Our interpretation of the metric refers to standard deviations as: $d = 0.2$ as small, $d = 0.4$ as medium, and $d = 0.6$ as large. One characteristic of these high-effect strategies is that they can be used to provide an opportunity for maximizing feedback to learners. In the previous chapter, we discussed setting goals and providing feedback ($d = 0.61$) by using a simple goal accounting template. The effect size for cooperative learning, including turn-and-talk type strategies, we found to be high ($d = 0.73$), and therefore a viable strategy to increase student-to-student feedback (Marzano et al., 2001, p. 87).

"I did not think of turn-and-talk when I read about cooperative learning strategy as a high-yield strategy, because I perceived cooperative learning as students working on projects in large groups," Ian said.

Also, when I first thought about incorporating turn-and-talk strategies, I immediately focused on the strategy as a teaching technique; that is, when and where I would be able to have time to fit it into my lesson. After we discussed the technique as a cue for students to have an opportunity repeatedly during class to focus on the topic of lesson, I became aware of how many times during a class students benefit cognitively. Over time, students began to ask for brief processing time during lectures.

**HINGES IN ACTION**

Peer discussion allows students to seek feedback for clarification and to generate questions. Peer discussion can also motivate students to practice producing useful feedback.

## FEEDBACK: PEER TEACHING

Ian Mulligan seemed pleased that the informal cooperative learning technique allowed students to evaluate each other and reteach, increasing feedback from student to peers, but also giving students time to reflect on their own understanding about the tasks tied to the curriculum standards and objectives. Grant Wiggins, known for extensive work in the area of performance assessment, writes about feedback on his blog, "Feedback is value-neutral help on worthy tasks. It describes what the learner did and did not do in relation to her goals. It is actionable information, and it empowers the student to make intelligent adjustments when she applies it to her next attempt to perform" (2010, para. 5).

Ian continued:

> Thinking about turn-and-talk strategies as a way for students to get feedback to know how well they are keeping up with the lecture changed it for me. I was surprised at how easily they interacted about the topic and how natural it was for me to ask them to redirect their attention to the front of the room. As soon as I saw a student or two look like he was not connecting with the material, I suggested a turn-and-talk. In the first class period that I tried it, I was honestly amazed at how obvious it became to me when students needed to process the information and what cue to use to get them to do it. It seemed a bit too easy, really.

He also noticed that students were more likely to ask for clarification from him during the class when they were given time to share with partners.

Probably what surprised Ian the most was how the feedback changed his teaching:

> It dawned on me while the students were talking, that I could walk around the tables with a roster of student names and "assess" the students using a simple scale like a 4-3-2-1 by just listening to their conversations. After two or three times, it became really important for me to listen, sometimes to provide my expertise, but also listen so I would know what they were discussing, providing feedback to me so I would know what to reteach!
>
> I recently had a conversation with another teacher about using pair-share in a high school class and she wondered if it was "awkward" for me to just cut the students loose into conversation during my lecture and then cut them off to come back to the group. My reply was a simple "yes."

It was a bit awkward, or maybe uncomfortable, but after a few days, the students coveted those times to process, make clarifications, and refocus, and I needed the stop times to informally assess individuals and the class.

When Ian shared his story, he laughed and mused, "Who would have thought that a soccer coach would think he needed a clipboard to walk around documenting data in a science classroom?" He uses a seating chart such as Figure 4.1, using a simple rubric so he can write in various scores or even a comment for the students as he conducts formative assessment.

Informal cooperative learning allowed the students the chance to peer teach and seek correction, but it gave the teacher the opportunity to deliberately interact with students multiple times during class. When necessary, Ian could provide expert feedback to students as he moved about the classroom.

Teachers use variations of the turn-and-talk to change the pairings so students interact with other students, such as cooperative learning structures recommended by Kagan and Kagan (2009). Some teachers prefer to change seating charts weekly so that the pairs change, or to use techniques such as the following:

1. *Clock partners.* Each student draws an analog clock with numbers. Students move about the room asking students to sign up with partner for a certain "time." When the teacher asks students to "find your 2 o'clock" partner, the students find each other to talk.

2. *2 × 2.* After students turn-and-talk, together they find another pair to discuss their findings, extending their discussion with another pair.

3. *Tripods.* Arrange students in groups of three so that one student can take the opportunity to seek information or give information to another group when needed.

**Figure 4.1** Ian Mulligan Scoring Seating Chart

Class:

Date:

Goal/objectives:

| | | | | | |
|---|---|---|---|---|---|
| Student name | Student name | Student name | Student name | Student name | Student name |
| Student name | Student name | Student name | Student name | Student name | Student name |
| Student name | Student name | Student name | Student name | Student name | Student name |
| Student name | Student name | Student name | Student name | Student name | Student name |
| Student name | Student name | Student name | Student name | Student name | Student name |

1 – Minimal understanding 2 – Basic 3 – Proficient 4 – Advanced

After partner sharing, the teacher may ask for a comment from each group, ask one group or one partner to go to the board, or use techniques such as passing index cards or sticky notes to gather words or questions from groups, reducing the class responses to a manageable number.

Ian's experience reviving cooperative learning seems to be another soup-and-ladle story. By using the turn-and-talk techniques strategically to increase information feedback, he created an environment for formative assessment. The teacher has the opportunity to give feedback to some learners while others talk, to assess and document student performances in order to differentiate instruction, and also to receive feedback from the students to make teaching decisions. When students are given the opportunity to turn-and-talk, they initiate feedback through peer teaching, ask questions that pertain to their own understandings, and gain the confidence to initiate feedback and instruction from the teacher.

As a high school science teacher, Ian Mulligan admitted afterward that he had been worried about taking up too much time, but realized later that when students sought and received peer feedback frequently in class, there were fewer interruptions or disruptions, and students stayed more focused so they actually covered material more deeply than before.

## PAUSE TO REFLECT

How can you use informal cooperative learning techniques such as turn-and-talk to increase engagement and deeper understanding?

How would you describe the formative assessment benefits?

## FEEDBACK: THE BRAIN THAT
## CHANGES ITSELF

Despite new information about how the brain works and why teachers should use new teaching strategies about feedback, many teachers seem somewhat reticent to try new strategies. It might be that brain science had inauspicious beginnings. Brain scientists in the 1800s, known as phrenologists, measured the shape and size of bumps on the head believed to be important to predict or explain character and intellect, but the discredited science left many believing that the brain was simply a black box or a *tabula rasa*. For the next sixty years of research on learning, techniques for improving human behaviors (think: teaching techniques) were based on behaviorism, dominated by B.F. Skinner, a Harvard psychologist. Behaviorists cared little about the brain or the mind because what was important to them was identifying the laws of behavior through an applied stimulus and the observed response. Yet, a dramatic shift in the definition of feedback occurred between the 1920s and the 1980s, a change from behaviorism to neuroscience.

Norman Doidge, MD, currently a psychoanalyst and researcher at Columbia University, writes enthusiastically about how the brain not only is not hardwired, but that it changes its own structure and function. He notes that Skinner's mentor, John B. Watson, was wrong about brain science, since Watson contemptuously wrote, "Most of the psychologists talk quite volubly about the formation of new pathways in the brain, as through there were a group of tiny servants of Vulcan there who run through the nervous system with hammer and chisel digging new trenches and deepening old ones" (as quoted in Doidge, 2007, p. 137).

The science of the behaviorists accurately described how people (and animals) respond to stimuli with physical responses. They were able to extend the simple idea of stimulus and response to create predictable scenarios, implying that the way a person makes improvement comes from feedback from an outside stimulus. Then neuroscientists came along showing that the inner workings of the brain are observable, just as the physical responses were observable to the behaviorists. Then neuroscientists saw feedback as strengthening neural pathways making memories. Neuroscience also confirms that the brain originates stimuli and does not need to wait for feedback from external sources. Not all of medical research is useful in schools, but enlarging the concept of feedback to include new information about how the brain changes itself seems timely.

Interestingly, much of the research on feedback since the 1970s has been dedicated to computer-assisted instruction. Software developers have spent considerable resources identifying how to incorporate feedback so that individual users remain motivated by the computer software and also see gains in content understanding or skills as a result. Since computer software intentionally reduces human interaction, some of their concerns do not translate to classrooms where teachers can mediate learning (Mason & Bruning, 2001). This research, coupled with neurological studies, will continue to expand the field and create useful information for schools.

Judy Willis, neurologist turned middle school teacher, wrote in 2006: "The more ways the material to be learned is introduced to the brain and reviewed, the more dendritic pathways of access will be created" (p. 4). She notes that a learner needs to use multiple ways to hold and manipulate new information in order to activate previously stored loops of knowledge and increase the likelihood that the information will be stored in long-term memory. In addition to more sensory strategies such as visuals or nonlinguistic representations, students also need the opportunity to use strategies in an environment where correction and elaboration can occur for individuals.

## PAUSE TO REFLECT

What does Judy Willis mean by indicating that a learner needs to use multiple pathways, and how does that relate to feedback?

We discussed goal setting and informal cooperative learning in previous sections. Adding to the list of nonnegotiable strategies is note taking, because in addition to providing learners an opportunity to write and think, it gives them the chance to interact about what they have written and understood. As mentioned previously, one characteristic of the high-effect strategies is that they provide an opportunity for maximizing feedback to learners. The effect size for note taking we found to be very high ($d = 1.00$) in *Classroom Instruction That Works* (Marzano et al., 2001, p. 44). Feedback during or after note taking gives learners the chance to verify and evaluate what they know, but also an opportunity to "continually add to the notes and revise them as their understanding of content deepens and sharpens" (p. 45).

## SIMPLE TECHNIQUE: TAKE NOTES

"Note taking used to be an option," seventh grade English teacher Becky Wegner said.

At the beginning of the semester I felt obligated to tell students to take notes during my presentations of the material, but I left it up to them. I knew that my students who were organized did well; the ones who neglected to bring notebooks or kept sloppy folders performed poorly. When I read the research on note-taking effectiveness, it confirmed my bias.

Jenny Hensgen, a seventh grade science teacher, told me:

> In my life science classroom, I always tried to find a balance between the inquiry, hands-on experiences, labs, and taking notes during a lecture or presentation of slides. In the past I delivered the notes using an overhead and later an electronic whiteboard to give students the main ideas found in the text, as well as other pertinent information not addressed in the book.
>
> Now I realize that the problem was that the students didn't interact with their notes; some of the students diligently copied the notes but didn't read them over, while others faked their note taking and certainly did not understand the underlying concepts.

Two topics became apparent to Becky and Jenny when we discussed their existing teaching practices and how they related to helping all students engage and perform better:

1. At least four or five students did not take notes well, even when they were projected on the screen. Those students, the tell-tale students, tended to perform poorly on tests. They needed direct instruction and different techniques.
2. The students viewed the notes as daily assignments, not works in progress to deepen understandings.

To teach seventh graders the value of note taking as a tool to seek informational feedback, all students also needed a practical but reliable way to organize and maintain an interactive notebook so that they could see the entire body of work that they create over the course of a unit or a semester. "These seemingly simple ideas became 'ah-moments' for me. I have begun to incorporate interactive notebooks. I am not sure how I missed the notion of 'interactive' and 'notebook' making the note taking a viable strategy for students to seek and receive feedback before, but it works now," Becky said. "This also reminds me that sometimes we have to use the simple, not fancy, techniques. It is like the cardboard and the mirrors that the neuroscientist Ramachandran used."

## FEEDBACK: SELF, PEER, TEACHER

According to Becky, many of her middle school students took notes as assignments, but were not used to keeping a notebook to use interactively, to seek feedback, during class. She focused on teaching students to:

1. Organize their notebooks by the standards and objectives to self-monitor, but also to efficiently request feedback and information from others (peers and teacher).

2. Learn and use different note-taking methods to organize the new information into useful formats so that seeking information from others or from other sources becomes highly productive.

3. Judge performance accurately and communicate with others efficiently to have the opportunity to improve. By using a basic rubric, communication could be purposeful.

## GOALS TO GUIDE NOTES

Becky teaches all of her students how to organize spiral notebooks for English class. In the first few pages of the notebook, students paste the standards so that when they are working on individual lessons, they can copy them from the list onto the page in the notebook where they take notes that day (see Figures 4.2–4.5).

**Figure 4.2** Notebook With Standards

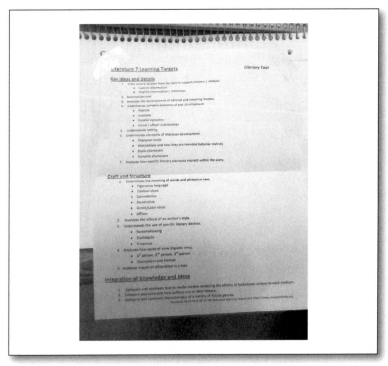

*Source:* Becky Wegner.

These are the goals, standards, and objectives that students have taped in their notebooks. We refer to these targets at the beginning of a quarter or beginning of a unit so students know where we are going.

Students are very familiar with those goals and have a copy of them inside their notebooks. In addition, I tell the students which objective we are learning about each day and we have conversations centered on those during the learning process. Students write the objective in their notebooks as a way to organize their notebooks. By providing students with this structure for learning, the students do not have to guess what they are actually supposed to be learning during the lesson and I don't have to guess what they already know.

The responses that I have obtained from students over the years regarding the objectives is overwhelmingly positive in that they like to know what they are supposed to learn that day, for a unit, quarter, or the year. Having the objectives in their notebooks allows the students to get a glimpse of their learning for the year and they can be referred to throughout the year. At the beginning of each quarter, the students open their notebooks to the standards and objectives and I map out the sequence that will be the focus of learning during that particular quarter.

## PAUSE TO REFLECT

If students learn to organize a notebook, in effect their own personal texts, do you think they will be more likely to participate in the instruction?

## NOTE-TAKING METHODS

Most students had some experience taking notes, but Becky provided direct instruction on note taking by accessing various websites on study skills. She showed students how an online search for note-taking strategies results in many examples and explanations, such as the outlining, webbing or mapping with graphic representations and pictorals, the Cornell method, and charting.

Depending on the goals for the lesson, the students used different methods. Becky indicates that changing methods was new to her because she remembered learning how to take outlining notes as a student in junior high. "If we are working on poems, we might take our notes using a web or a mind map, but if we are

**Figure 4.3** Note-Taking Method 1. This notebook page shows how a student recorded the objective, as well as a score for understanding and effort.

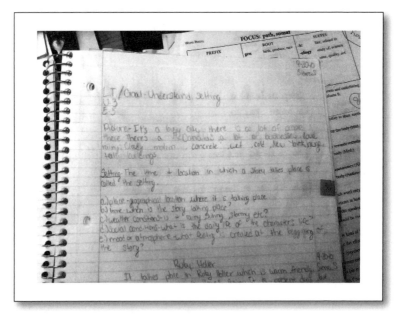

*Source:* Becky Wegner.

reading informational text, we use the Cornell method because it emphasizes new terms or phrases," she explained. After a few weeks of instruction, all students became more motivated to take notes because using multiple methods allowed them flexibility to organize and discuss new material. She increased opportunities for students to process aloud with table partners to verify task activity and to provide corrective comments.

Methods such as charting and mapping lend themselves to discussion, so students began to take the opportunity to check with each other to extend ideas, rather than complete assignments just to be finished.

**Figure 4.4**   Note-Taking Method 2. This student used a graphic
organizer to chart information to prepare for an
assignment about cause and effect.

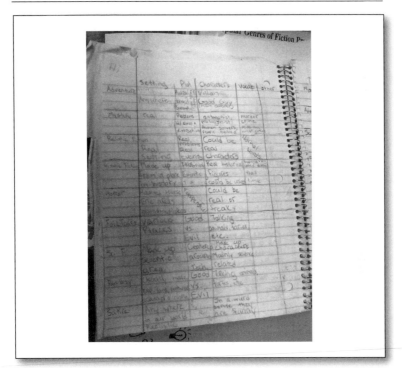

*Source:* Becky Wegner.

Becky adds:

> I sometimes use the notebooks as an exit slip. For example, if
> students have to make a generalization about their learning,
> I will read what the students write before they are allowed
> to leave the classroom. When students know their note-
> books are important to me, they are more apt to engage in
> the learning process and become successful.

Since Becky became motivated to ensure that all students
organized their notebooks well, it became a vehicle for

**Figure 4.5** Note-Taking Method 3. This note-taking method is a variation on the Cornell method.

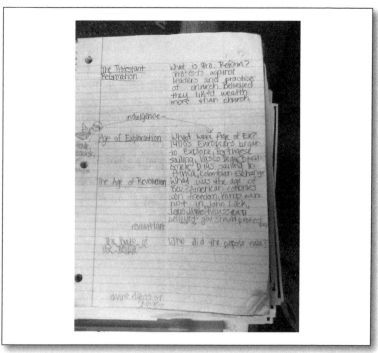

*Source:* Becky Wegner.

communicating with each other and with her. Becky noticed changes in her students' learning habits:

1. Sharing notes with peers increased overall class productivity and engaged individual learners who previously gave up when required to copy notes.

2. Student notes became works in progress, not assignments, so homework extended schoolwork purposefully for class the next day.

3. Students brought their notebooks because of pride for their work and reported that their parents were pleased with the quality of their notes, too.

## PAUSE TO REFLECT

Do you notice that different people take notes differently? What techniques do you use when you need to remember information?

## EVALUATION SCALE OR RUBRIC

In addition to making sure that students could seek help if they needed to do so, Becky taught them how to incorporate a U (understanding) score and an E (effort) score for the notes based on the objectives using the following five-point rubric or scale:

5 = an above and beyond level of understanding

4 = a solid understanding

3 = a basic understanding

2 = a limited understanding

1 = no understanding

At the beginning of each lesson, the students scored themselves both for personal monitoring, but also to give feedback to Becky as she walked around the room.

Engagement is a means to achievement. In my class, the student's notebook is an important tool for engagement. The notebook is where the student writes the informational type notes about the objective, but also reflects on learning. In addition, students get feedback from me or another student about the contents of their notebooks. Sometimes we write the feedback in the notebook and at other times give verbal feedback that students can record or use to correct their work. They want, actually the students seem to crave, the individualized recognition.

Once Becky realized that for middle school students the notebook became an interactive tool, she and the students began to use it to communicate with others.

> Students can look back into their notes to make sure they are using the newly acquired information to guide their learning. When I walk around the room while students are working, I hear and see students referring back to their notes when talking with their peers. I encourage students to adjust their notes if they discover that they missed something that would help them with their learning.
>
> The students begin to self-regulate their understanding and monitor their progress through the use of the notebooks and the feedback that is given to them. The notebooks are a great way to increase student engagement, ultimately increasing student learning. I have seen their growth and, more importantly, the students themselves have seen their growth in learning.

## PAUSE TO REFLECT

Do students in your school learn to take notes differently in different classes? Should some of the techniques be uniform across the school or should every teacher give different options to students?

## FEEDBACK IS A TWO-WAY STREET

Jenny Hensgen realized that taking notes could become a priority for her students if she made it a priority to teach it.

> I started teaching students how to take notes when I realized that it would increase engagement and achievement if I took the time to model and practice different techniques. For students who struggled to find main ideas and important information, I gave them transparencies and a washable fine-lined

marker. They placed the transparency over the section they read and underlined the information they thought applied to the goal. Using this strategy I was able to quickly check the underlining of the important information.

I now get feedback about all students' comprehension, which allows me to readjust or differentiate materials and how I present information. I can give students feedback about the notes and information they need to meet the goal. I don't assume that students are coming to seventh grade knowing how to read technical information or nonfiction and believe that the reading and note-taking strategies need to be taught every year.

Since I expect the students to make some new meaning about the information they have gathered, students compare notes with each other and ask each other questions about what they have written. When they justify why they have written specific things down and how it relates to the goal, they learn to give and receive feedback from fellow students.

Students want to show me their thinking in order to receive feedback, but I gain feedback that drives my instruction. I get immediate feedback about the clarity of my presentations or lectures based on the level that the students show in their notes that they understand the information. These behaviors are becoming automatic in my room. Questions from the students and class discussions have become more on topic and meaningful for everyone now that I recognize note taking as a technique to remember information, but also to seek and receive feedback from others.

Jenny and Becky each believe they are soup-and-ladle teachers because all of the pieces were there, but they knew that a few students were not learning. Until they conceptualized note taking as a source for feedback, the hinge factor, between teacher and student and back again, they had accepted poor student work as part of teaching. In their cases, the "invisible in plain sight" tool of interactive notebooks was used by some, but not all, students. Both teachers had to decide to change their expectations for all students, their teaching, and how they could adjust to engage all students.

## PAUSE TO REFLECT

How would interactive notebooks help some of the disengaged students in your building?

## PUTTING IT TOGETHER

Cheryl Spalter, a fifth grade teacher, looks reserved and very petite, but I would follow her down any dark alley since she is also a P90X trainer. You might recognize P90X from the infomercials by Tony Horton, who flexes his muscles enthusiastically encouraging viewers to Decide! Commit! Succeed! When Cheryl showed me her before-and-after pictures, my jaw dropped. Now that is someone who can decide, commit, and succeed when she wants to. So it was no surprise that she changed her instructional strategies.

After a morning workshop on instructional strategies, Cheryl approached me to admit that she had attended the workshop reluctantly because she was considered a good teacher and only had a few students who did not perform well based on test scores, but got increasingly excited about improving student learning because it reminded her of the exercise regime.

Prior to attending your workshops, I "thought" I was a good teacher. Honestly, data has shown over time that my most of my students have shown significant growth on state assessments, so I figured, I must be teaching well enough; why change what's not broken? However, my personal attitude now is that what works can always be improved upon. The techniques you showed us have made me change my professional view today. I am kind of embarrassed to say that I never thought about the classroom from the student point of view, but now it makes a lot of sense.

Cheryl became more deliberate about using a goal accounting template for student self-feedback and student-to-teacher feedback, and boosted informal cooperative learning for student-to-student feedback to clarify and correct misconceptions and notes. What surprised Cheryl was that those three strategies created the environment for better questions.

In the past, my students might see the objective for the lesson on the board but then I'd go right into teaching the new information. Now, at the beginning of the lesson, after they fill out their goal sheets, I ask students a thought-provoking question about the objective or cue them to generate a question about it with peers before discussing as a whole group.

Although her students were seated in groups and she let them work together at certain times, Cheryl said she had never used informal cooperative learning as a way to increase student engagement, and therefore learning.

As the teacher, this has helped me tremendously because I'm immediately cued into misconceptions from all students, not just the few who may have responded in a "cold call." This one small tweak has opened up a whole new world in my class. Now I can adjust my lesson to clarify those misunderstandings. Never before did I consider asking them what they knew about a math, science, or social studies topic. Today, if I don't ask my students to pair up to generate questions, they will prompt me to do so. They truly want to share with me how much they know and are honest in discussing where they have limited knowledge.

As Cheryl found out, students could ask higher order questions when they knew the goal for the lesson, kept interactive notebooks, and were provided time and direction to share their ideas with partners for correction as well as elaboration. She tells her students to decide, commit, and succeed on the standards and objectives now by asking questions, interacting with peers, and tracking their progress with her help.

## MANY STRATEGIES WORK

Many teaching techniques are powerful for learners, but the ones described in this chapter tend to be strategies that are "invisible in plain sight" and should be used to maximize feedback for all students. Teachers and students were using some of the strategies, but until they connected them to increasing feedback and student engagement, they had not been motivated deliberately and purposefully to use them to progress on standards and objectives. Many other teaching and learning strategies can also be adapted so that they provide opportunities for learners to know their performance relative to the aim or goal and provide informational feedback for incremental growth.

The next chapter discusses a view of feedback that focuses on teacher-to-student feedback and standards-based record keeping.

### PAUSE TO REFLECT

How would you conduct staff development to introduce cooperative learning, note taking, and questioning as engagement strategies?

Would observations change as a result of the information about watching the students for opportunities for feedback in addition to watching teachers use high-yield strategies?

# CHAPTER FIVE

# FEEDBACK FROM THE TEACHER

A drianne Braxton is a one of those teachers you love to observe. She seems so nice and genteel with classroom management entirely based on a few "looks." When Adrianne looks in one direction or another, the students know exactly what it means. She just has that teaching gift. With such a command of the classroom, Adrianne still had some students who disengaged during lessons. She made no excuses for her students based on socioeconomics or environment; she just thought that if they engaged better during instruction they would perform better on the common assessments given by the district every six weeks.

When I observed Adrianne, it became clear that she gave feedback to students during instruction but it was spontaneous and never recorded, so she had little chance of remembering the information either for individual student assessment, noticing patterns of learning to adjust instruction, or for differentiation. She had provided the goal derived from the Kentucky state standards and planned a lesson that included both direct instruction and time for application, but while the students worked she walked around the room helping. In one class, she seemed to reteach a procedure four times at different tables. I am not proud to be known as the person who recommended that we stop helping children in school, but in her case, that was my suggestion.

In *Transformative Assessment,* Jim Popham defines formative assessment as representing evidence-based instructional decision making, and he states, "So, even if there were not a shred of empirical evidence to support the worth of formative assessment in the classroom, I would still be advocating its use because it makes so darn much sense!" (2008, p. 7). In Adrianne's class, changing her purpose of walking around the room from only helping and reteaching students to deliberately adding observing and providing formative feedback to students became practical formative assessment.

## FEEDBACK BY WALKING AROUND

The simple tool, nothing fancy in this case, was a clipboard, roster of student names, and the goal or objective for the lesson (see Figure 5.1), much like the one that science teacher Ian Mulligan used in Chapter 4.

Once she completed the instruction and gave the directions for a task, Adrianne circled the room with her roster, scoring students on the lesson goal, based on peering over their shoulders. As she moved around the room, she interacted briefly to clarify and give specific feedback to students based on the goal of the lesson. After one loop around the room, she noticed that various students had made the same error so she asked the class to stop working for a brief reteach.

At the end of the first class, Adrianne beamed. She realized that for the first time, she knew how well every student knew the goal and she knew what to adjust for the next lesson, rather than just thinking about moving on to the next lesson. Students were engaged because with the clipboard, she became ubiquitous, not

**Figure 5.1**    Teacher Scoring Document

| Week of: _____ |||||||
| :-- | :-- | :-- | :-- | :-- | :-- | :-- |
| Goals: _____ |||||||
| Rubric: 1—Basic   2—Minimal   3—Proficient   4—Advanced (use + and −) |||||||
| **Student Names** | | | | | | **Overall Score** |
| | | | | | | |
| | | | | | | |
| | | | | | | |
| | | | | | | |
| | | | | | | |
| | | | | | | |
| | | | | | | |
| | | | | | | |
| | | | | | | |
| | | | | | | |
| | | | | | | |
| | | | | | | |
| | | | | | | |
| | | | | | | |
| | | | | | | |
| | | | | | | |
| | | | | | | |
| | | | | | | |
| | | | | | | |
| | | | | | | |
| | | | | | | |
| | | | | | | |
| | | | | | | |
| | | | | | | |
| | | | | | | |
| | | | | | | |
| | | | | | | |

just tethered to providing help to one group. At the end of the day, Adrianne acknowledged that she had collected standards-based data for all of her students that day in various subject areas, knew exactly what to adjust, and she wasn't tired!

Walking around the room with a scoring roster as students work independently may not be a practice every teacher uses, but the suggestion to do so increases teacher-to-student feedback. In some cases, the teacher gives corrections, and at the same time acknowledges student work that shows progress toward the goal. As she walks around, students are more likely to seek her attention or help when she approaches them—they stay more engaged.

As we met over the year, we devised various techniques about using the standards-based clipboard and giving students feedback while walking around:

1. Prepare the rosters for the week. Leave enough spaces for daily scores for objectives, but also for an overall score for the standards.

2. Use a different, color-coded clipboard for each subject area.

3. Never erase. Every data point can inform the trend.

4. Use a simple scale such as 1 to 4 (with pluses or minuses) and make a mental note that everyone is a "3" unless he or she gets a score. That saves on time writing and on looking at the chart after.

5. Share scores with students as a quick way to give feedback in every class.

6. Move around the room two or three times, scoring before interacting with students, to give them a chance to work before interrupting their independent attempts to perform.

7. If you have the "answer" sheet on your clipboard, too, you can sometimes have the papers "graded" before students leave the class.

**PAUSE TO REFLECT**

How does this example of assessing and feedback during instruction increase student engagement? How does this example of assessment during instruction help the teacher?

## FEEDBACK TO STANDARDS

In the example above, the teacher used a score sheet similar to students using the goal accounting template in Chapter 3. Standards-based scoring is the common characteristic for both of the forms. In each case, the student and the teacher evaluate performance based on the curriculum standard or objective, leaving open the possibility for multiple opportunities to learn new information and practice activities tied to the standard. These informal formative assessment techniques require small changes in resources and time but generate achievement gains because they are practical ways that feedback moves from the teacher to the student and back again based on a common goal.

When Adrianne Braxton and the other teachers in her building were introduced to using a standards-based grading software program that would generate standards-based report cards, they easily and confidently added daily and weekly data based on their walk-around-classroom assessments and tests. When it came time to produce a report card, all of their data were collected by the standards with averages and trends.

As she reflects back to her practices before, Adrianne notes that individual students must not have received very much feedback from her other than praise. "I still praise my students a lot," she said. "That is because they are doing really well and we know it based on our data!"

## PAUSE TO REFLECT

Has your school introduced standards-based report cards without practicing standards-based assessment and record keeping?

In his *Assessment Manifesto,* Rick Stiggins called for a more balanced assessment system nationally, writing that the quality of assessments have indeed become stronger with more fidelity to standards and the dependability of the resulting scores, yet, "quality must also include the impact of the scores on the learner *during the learning*" (2008, p. 2).

Assessment during the learning implies that students receive feedback during the instructional part of the lesson. That way they may identify errors and become aware of misconceptions while in the exact environment to receive additional information, relevant cues, and elaboration. The previous chapters offered strategies for students to assess themselves in order to seek elaboration and peer assessment. This chapter focuses on how teachers, in classrooms with thirty students, may assess during the learning. Since most teachers are providing as much feedback as they think they can, grading as many papers as they believe possible, this chapter is mostly about changing habits during instruction, or ladling the soup differently in class.

## HINGES IN ACTION

Ongoing assessment during instruction, or formative assessment, offers the student an opportunity to increase performance methodically, maximizing efficiency. Documenting formative assessment gives the teacher a reliable record of all students' performances to increase the possibility of systematically providing instructional opportunities for every student.

The cornerstone of assessment during learning is having a good curriculum document so teachers use informal standards-based assessment during class to save time, give more accurate formative feedback, and differentiate when necessary. In the previous example, an elementary teacher changed her "helping time" to assessment during learning, during which she provides specific feedback to students but uses their performance data as feedback to adjust her instruction. The next example, about a high school English department, extends the notion of informally assessing students by adopting a standards-based approach to daily and ongoing assignments. A third example shows how a math department aligns all assessments to standards and provides feedback and reteaching opportunities to students, who make tremendous gains. In the final example, a music teacher shares his transformation, even though his first reaction was that he already gives feedback and there are too many students for the teacher to provide individual feedback. In each case, the feedback to the students from the teacher has changed from feedback to tasks to expert feedback about performances on curriculum goals.

In the next section, high school English teachers become the positive deviants in the school when they use an electronic program to track all assignments and assessments by standards. In the process they build a new culture of improvement because the feedback teachers offer to students gives verification by standards, but encourages elaboration since the assessment occurs during the learning. Changing the way that they grade students to scoring and tracking performances by standards provides the missing link to formative assessment, because multiple scores tie to topics while giving the chance for future instruction. In addition, teachers seek technology solutions to improve the efficiency of providing feedback to learners.

## DOCTORS, PILOTS, AND
## ENGLISH TEACHERS

In his book *Super Crunchers*, Ian Ayres (2007) writes about a doctor who worked with a software developer to create a software program, a super cruncher, that would allow doctors to electronically communicate about symptoms, responses, and ultimately cures. The algorithms, which involve surprisingly few critical factors, combine speed, size, and scale of data to predict a few solutions. The doctor's motivation was a three-year-old patient misdiagnosed with chicken pox, who actually suffered a rare flesh-eating virus. The Isabel Program was named after the child, who survived, and it manages vast amounts of data that doctors use to consider new alternatives as solutions. Technology allows rapid digitalization of information and the designers note that computers are better at remembering information than people are. The doctor and parent of the child successfully created the evidence-based program for physicians. Seems like a case of positive deviance.

The doctor and developer donated the software, but to their dismay, other doctors did not accept the software as a way to reduce misdiagnoses. Doctors responded that they were more comfortable using their own diagnostic procedures. Ayres continues relating his story about the power of technology, databases, and the social complexity.

The same doctor later started learning to fly and he observed that pilots passionately accepted training and support software with no misgivings. Asked why pilots, and not the highly educated doctors, accepted support software so keenly, the flight instructor noted, "It's very simple. Unlike pilots, doctors don't go down with their planes" (Ayres, 2007, p. 101).

One is led to believe that the doctors' resistance to using the software has more to do with the fact that making changes to habits is difficult, even though strategies are "invisible in plain sight." Changing habits is not easy.

Trent Scott, an English department chairperson, knows about changing habits. His school district rolled out a plan for standards-based learning by providing a software program. First-year and veteran teachers alike implemented the software, but found that in order to use it they had to change their teaching and assessment habits.

## A GOOD SET OF GOALS

Similar to the experience teachers in Chapter 4 had, when creating the goal accounting templates, standards-based record keeping requires a good set of goals. In the book, *Improving Student Learning One Teacher at a Time* (Pollock, 2007), I describe a protocol to unpack standards so that they follow the Goldilocks rule: not too general, not too specific, but "just right." When a teacher or school produces the just-right standards, they are used in the goal accounting templates so students can reflect on their own performances, on the teacher clipboard forms so teachers can provide goal-based feedback to students, and in an electronic gradebook to view the data over time to see trends by individual and class.

In a standards-based grading program, the teacher opens "new assignment" and selects an appropriate standard(s). The process is similar to writing an e-mail message: when opening a new message, the writer selects the address or addresses to which the message will be sent. The software can organize the assignments by chronology or by standards, depending on the report.

In traditional grading, the teacher selects categories of assignments (e.g., homework, class work, practice, quiz, test, or project). Using that system, students may see the progression of assignment scores over time, but do not necessarily see growth in skills or understandings about topics. In addition, teachers, unable to see the progress by the standards or topics, tend not to differentiate or make instructional decisions based on data. Experience shows that students and teachers are rarely motivated by the data in traditional categories to improve, as much as they value completed assignments.

## PREPARE TO GIVE FEEDBACK

The best advice I can give to teachers willing to create an environment for increased feedback in a classroom is to prepare to give feedback. The templates, the techniques, and the software are great tools, but preparing the curriculum goals is paramount to daily feedback and viewing performance over time to provide useful feedback to students.

When Trent Scott's department volunteered to use the software, they did so because they expressed dissatisfaction about student performances, especially in writing, and it seemed like an opportunity to sharpen the saw. Before moving ahead, Trent and his staff examined their document: "Entirely cumbersome and suffering from a serious collection of standards bloat!" He wrote:

> The most important part of this process, after building our foundation in the efficacy and necessity of standards-based learning, was working through our standards and benchmarks (some groups call them standards and objectives or sometimes standards and indicators) in order to revise them for clarity and efficiency. If I were to advise any department (regardless of curriculum) on where to start, it would be here. By rolling up our sleeves and digging into the benchmarks, unpacking them and sifting through the verbiage, we were able to discern which were truly valuable and assessable. By the time the work was done, we had reduced the overall number of benchmarks to a far more manageable number. There is no such thing as good feedback to a bad set of goals.

**Figure 5.2** English Standards

---

*ENGLISH STANDARDS AND BENCHMARKS 9–12*

**48 Benchmarks**

**Standard 1: Use reading strategies to understand text.**

**1.12.1** Use a variety of strategies to extend reading vocabulary.
**1.12.2** Understand specific devices that convey meaning.
**1.12.3** Use strategies to extend comprehension.

**Standard 2: Critically analyze text.**

**2.12.1** Analyze author technique in the context of history and culture.
**2.12.2** Understand how universal themes are developed in literature.
**2.12.3** Understand how literary elements combine to produce a dominant tone, effect, or theme.

**Standard 3: Read to acquire information.**

**3.12.1** Integrate information from multiple sources when developing a position on a topic.
**3.12.2** Evaluate the reliability and authenticity of information.
**3.12.3** Understand and follow written directions.

**Standard 4: Use the general skills and strategies of the writing process.**

**4.12.1** Use a variety of prewriting strategies.
**4.12.2** Develop a composition through a series of drafts, using revision strategies.
**4.12.3** Use strategies to address writing to different audiences and purposes.

**Standard 5: Use the stylistic and rhetorical aspects of writing.**

**5.12.1** Use a clear thesis and effective organization of supporting ideas to communicate knowledge, opinions, and insights.
**5.12.2** Use precise and descriptive language that clarifies and enhances ideas and supports different purposes.

*(Continued)*

**Figure 5.2** (Continued)

**5.12.3** Use paragraph form in writing.
**5.12.4** Use a variety of sentence structures and lengths.
**5.12.5** Use a variety of transitional devices.
**5.12.6** Use a variety of techniques to convey a personal style and voice.

**Standard 6: Use grammatical and mechanical conventions.**

**6.12.1** Use conventions of standard English in written compositions.
**6.12.2** Use conventions of spelling in written compositions.
**6.12.3** Use conventions of capitalization in written compositions.
**6.12.4** Use conventions of punctuation in written compositions.
**6.12.5** Use appropriate format in writing.
**6.12.6** Use correct tenses to indicate the relative order and relationship of events.
**6.12.7** Use correct agreement.

**Standard 7: Gather and use information for research purposes.**

**7.12.1** Develop a focused topic.
**7.12.2** Use a variety of sources to gather information.
**7.12.3** Use a variety of criteria to evaluate the validity and reliability of primary and secondary source information.
**7.12.4** Synthesize information from multiple research studies to draw conclusions.
**7.12.5** Use systematic strategies to organize and record information.
**7.12.6** Present findings in a written format.
**7.12.7** Use standard format and methodology for documenting reference sources.

**Standard 8: Use listening and speaking strategies for different purposes.**

**8.12.1** Participate effectively in discussion.
**8.12.2** Use a variety of strategies to enhance listening comprehension and follow oral directions.
**8.12.3** Adjust message wording to particular audiences and for particular purposes.

**8.12.4** Develop and deliver presentations to convey information and ideas in a logical fashion.

**8.12.5** Use a variety of nonverbal delivery techniques for presentations.

**8.12.6** Participate effectively in question-and-answer sessions following presentations.

**8.12.7** Understand how style and content of spoken language varies in different contexts.

**8.12.8** Use feedback and self-evaluation to improve oral communication.

**8.12.9** Interpret literary works orally, citing textual data in support of assertions.

**Standard 9: Use viewing skills and strategies to understand and interpret visual media.**

**9.12.1** Use a range of strategies to interpret visual media.

**9.12.2** Use a variety of criteria to evaluate informational media.

**9.12.3** Understand how images and sound convey messages in visual media.

**9.12.4** Understand how literary forms can be represented in visual narratives.

**9.12.5** Understand that media messages have economic, political, social, and aesthetic purposes.

**Standard 10: Use technology to acquire, organize, and communicate information.**

**10.12.1** Use various technologies to present information.

**10.12.2** Communicate using online sources to exchange information.

English is perhaps the perfect model for standards-based learning as we are a spiraling curriculum. We essentially introduce and assess all of the same skills and standards over the course of a student's four-year high school career, just at varying levels of sophistication and maturation. When students do not receive adequate feedback, they can repeat the same mistakes for four years and that disengages them. As such, the next step in our process of implementing and assessing these forty-eight benchmarks seemed somewhat intuitive. We needed to investigate ways to instruct to these standards as well as give specific feedback for all of our students.

## PAUSE TO REFLECT

Once more, teachers identify the cornerstone of achievement may be a good set of curriculum standards that teachers and students use in class every day. What standards do teachers use in your school?

The importance of good standards documents cannot be overemphasized. Although standards documents at state levels or national levels may be too long or too short, the important characteristic is whether the feedback to the learner will motivate the student to perform and provide the teacher a criterion to which to create various assignments or assessments. In my experience, the average number of grade or course-level standards is about forty-five statements per subject area, as indicated in the document in Figure 5.2. Each of the statements can be further unpacked for more specificity.

In accordance with preparing to give feedback, it is important to emphasize the importance of aligning specific benchmarks and skills into units, pacing units, and really questioning the rationale of the standards. They have to lend themselves to deep understandings and discussions by both the first- and second-year teachers, as well as to veteran teachers who were open and eager to change instruction and assessment. Once they had their units organized, Trent explained the importance of "rubricizing" the assessments:

In other words, assessments (of writings, of projects, of oral presentations) were aligned to standards. This was such a valuable process, as it demanded the individual teacher to really consider how and why he or she was instructing and assessing a specific benchmark (course-level standard).

Teachers began to work together to polish assessment rubrics, compare notes, and garner more consistency. The fear, prior to the beginning of this process, was that teachers would become "robots" as we all fought to check off which benchmarks we had fulfilled. Instead, we are gaining a great deal of group wisdom as we created common assessments. As I have said before, we have different ways of skinning the cat through classroom instruction, but the cat always ends up skinned!

The assessments still gauge a student's proficiency in the skills required by the unit. We have gotten to the point, as professionals, when we can sit and share our student work to "ground ourselves" into the assessment rubric and what it means. Even us "old dogs" gain quite a bit of knowledge by going through this process and really asking questions of the rubrics and the work.

## PAUSE TO REFLECT

How does the English department experience compare to your experience with curriculum revision? The process may be similar, but are the expectations for implementation similar?

## BETTER FEEDBACK, BETTER PERFORMANCE

What matters to the teachers is whether they can succeed in improving student achievement. When asked about test scores, Trent indicates that they did make about a 7 percent gain, but he also emphasized that the importance was that all students are better writers and readers!

This has made the most difference in the instruction and assessment of writing. Whether it's a short paragraph response or a 20-page research paper, standards-based learning has made a significant difference. Once upon a time, writing instruction and enhancement seemed to be a mystery, especially to students who thought they were not good writers. What standards-based record keeping does is pull the shroud off of the skill, removes subjectivity, and clearly articulates for both the writer and the teacher what is expected.

When a student receives a writing prompt, there is a specific rubric attached explaining what proficiency looks like in the different standards areas. Instruction, then, is also demystified, as teachers are able to aim a student toward the standards areas with great specificity.

The degree to which this has helped my new instructors quickly find a comfort zone in teaching writing is unbelievable. To have resources (we share all of our rubrics through a common folder on the district server and also have a "mother rubric" for writing) available, as well as collegiate coaching and modeling, makes the teaching of writing far less daunting.

## FEEDBACK IN THE TWENTY-FIRST CENTURY

One of the unexpected, but welcomed, aspects of using the electronic standards-based record keeping is that it paved the way for the teachers in the department to expand to using another software program to give students individualized standards-based feedback. Trent's department began to use Turnitin (see Turnitin.com), a writing clearinghouse that allows them to collect work electronically and, using a grading feature, gives teachers the opportunity to insert comments and feedback directly onto an electronic version of a student's paper. Though they originally purchased the program to detect plagiarism, Trent's department has changed the emphasis so they can provide feedback to students and the result is that previously disengaged students receive more feedback than ever before. He describes the program as

> featuring a variety of comment palettes that speed up the feedback process and allow for even greater depth. Lastly, we can create assessment rubrics and then allow students to revise through the feedback and assessment. The greatest gains are made, obviously, through revision. Revision is the sign of feedback, lots and lots of feedback.

Trent asked students to describe the feedback they receive using the writing program based on the standards:

Electronically submitting our papers through this system allows for our teachers to give us very specific feedback, allowing for very efficient revisions as well as a reference for future papers.—S.

My favorite aspect is that it gives teachers the tool to give us electronic feedback. I like this because I know exactly which part of my paper they are commenting on, and it gives them more room to write so they can give me more feedback and they don't have to scribble something into the margins. Also, before using Turnitin, I hadn't had the opportunity of an online discussion board, which is unfortunate because it is such a useful tool. Not only can we take our literary analytical discussion outside of the classroom, we can get a deeper insight into the thoughts and ideas of our fellow classmates which we do not always get to do in classroom discussion, due to time constraints.—J.

The ability to read comments online and have those comments available to access for future reference has really helped me. Having all of the work I have done in one database has enhanced my writing techniques. Being able to trace comments throughout papers has been a large benefit, For example, realizing that I was missing the same benchmark, making the same mistakes over and over again was more recognizable through comments directly on the papers I had submitted. The ability to exchange information with classmates is also extremely beneficial. I even feel as though it benefits us in class discussions.—L.

After a while the specific, pinpointed comments started to get to me, and I found out that I wouldn't be able to just get through this year on the mediocre writing skills I had gathered so far. This effect, though probably not an intended function of the program, motivated me. When you physically hand in a printed essay, it's much easier to shove it in the back of your folder when it comes back to you, all red and marked up with comments.—L.

As Trent and his department look back on the five years that they have tracked student achievement to the standards, he notes that the entire process can be summed up in one word: feedback. He observes that in the past they had revised curriculums and even tried to use different software, but never saw the teachers or students motivated to integrate either into their habits.

"Once we began to discuss curriculum revision and software as ways to prepare and implement better feedback to students, the game changed." He wrote, "I can't honestly remember how I evaluated and provided feedback to my students before making the shift. In all honesty, I really don't want to remember and I'd never go back!"

## PAUSE TO REFLECT

How do the student responses indicate the importance of feedback both in terms of the standards-based feedback and the timing or frequency of teacher feedback?

## FEEDBACK AND THE UNMOTIVATED STUDENT

In an essay about formative assessment, Black and William wrote, "A focus on standards and accountability that ignores the processes of teaching and learning in classrooms will not provide the direction that teachers need in their quest to improve" (1998, p. 1). They continue, "Teachers need to know about their pupils' progress and difficulties with learning so that they can adapt their own work to meet pupils' needs—needs that are often unpredictable and that vary from one pupil to another" (p. 2).

Although the perceived need for standards-based grading emerged to improve low performers' achievement, teachers share experiences about using the protocol to improve learning for all students.

Betsy Bunting, high school math teacher, said:

As a teacher I have been particularly frustrated trying to achieve good results with two types of students. The unmotivated student and those who process slowly; both groups have been the least responsive to changes in curriculum, lesson planning, and learning activities. It seemed that no matter what I changed, I didn't see much improvement in their effort and/or understanding.

Every semester I try to inspire, threaten, and cajole underachieving kids into producing quality work. It has been an endless battle that I often lose. I just couldn't convince kids who were able to get passing grades doing poor quality work that it was worth the effort to do more work when all they achieved was a higher grade which they didn't care about anyway. On the flip side of that, I have seen good students who are obviously tired of seeing others get away with doing so little that they begin to question why they bother to work so hard.

In her high school, the math department agreed to change their grading practices in an effort to increase teacher feedback to students during the learning. They intended to improve individual math performances, but also to make program improvements. First, they revised their math curriculum documents so the curriculum statements were portable for posting on the board for each lesson and for aligning assessments in gradebooks. Betsy indicated that using a procedure similar to the one described in Chapter 3, they reduced their documents from an unruly 100+ statements to a clear set of approximately forty-five course or grade level standards, as shown in Figure 5.3.

**Figure 5.3**   Algebra Standards

| Number | Title |
|--------|-------|
| A.1 | Understand and apply the order of operations. |
| A.2 | Identify and apply algebraic properties. |
| A.3 | Interpret and compare scatter plots and correlation. |
| A.4 | Order and compare real numbers. |
| A.5 | Using real numbers to verify or refute conjectures. |
| A.6 | Classify and order real numbers. |
| A.7 | Solve basic equations. |
| A.8 | Solve multistep equations. |

| Number | Title |
| --- | --- |
| A.9 | Solve for a variable (literal equations). |
| A.10 | Real-world applications of linear functions. |
| A.11 | Represent linear functions in multiple ways. |
| A.12 | Recognize and use graphs of relations as functions. |
| A.13 | Identify patterns and write formulas for arithmetic sequences. |
| A.14 | Understand the concepts of slope and rate of change. |
| A.15 | Analyze linear functions using graphs, tables, and equations. |
| A.16 | Graph linear equations using slope. |
| A.17 | Write linear equations using slope intercept form. |
| A.18 | Graph linear functions involving absolute value. |
| A.19 | Solve basic inequalities. |
| A.20 | Solve basic equations involving absolute value. |
| A.21 | Graph linear inequalities. |
| A.22 | Solve systems of linear equations. |
| A.23 | Solve systems of equations using elimination. |
| A.24 | Real-world applications of basic equations. |
| A.25 | Real-world applications of basic inequalities. |
| A.26 | Real-world applications of linear systems. |
| B.1 | Multiply and divide monomials. |
| B.2 | Add and subtract polynomials. |
| B.3 | Multiply polynomials. |
| B.4 | Factor by grouping and GCF. |
| B.5 | Factor trinomials. |
| B.6 | Factor completely. |
| B.7 | Solve quadratic equations by factoring. |
| B.8 | Solve quadratic equations by graphing. |

*(Continued)*

**Figure 5.3** (Continued)

| Number | Title |
|--------|-------|
| B.9 | Analyze quadratic functions using graphs, tables, and equations. |
| B.10 | Real-world applications of quadratic functions. |
| B.11 | Distinguish between linear, quadratic, and exponential functions. |
| B.12 | Real-world applications of exponential equations. |
| B.13a | Simplify radicals. |
| B.13b | Operations on radicals. |
| B.14 | Radical applications. |
| B.15 | Basic matrix operations. |
| B.16 | Permutations and combinations. |
| B.17 | Probability distributions. |
| B.18 | Identify patterns and write formulas for geometric sequences. |
| C.1 | Interpret presented data. |
| C.2 | Calculate and analyze measures of central tendency. |
| C.3 | Calculate probability. |
| C.4 | Set up and solve ratios and proportions. |

Betsy describes her experience:

The students were frustrated and so was I. I decided to try standards-based grading since it was obvious that what I was currently doing did not work for these students. So I jumped in, mid-year, and gave it a shot. The results have been remarkable.

I piloted the program in my geometry classes. I assigned each unit a set of between four and seven standards that were the core concepts the student should know well by the end of the unit and graded each standard using the same terminology shown on the state tests: Advanced (five out of five correct, scores as 100%), Proficient (four out of five correct, scores as 93% or lowest possible A), Basic (three out of five correct, scores as 85% or lowest possible B), or Not Proficient (scores as 0%). If a unit had only a few standards, I pulled previous skill sheets to fill out the test and make sure they were retaining the skills.

I isolated harder skills, for example: solving backwards from area, which lower-achieving kids generally avoid on tests, as individual standards rather than just higher-level problems. I also clearly stated on the test if any problems in the standard did not have supporting work and, if required, an explanation, a Not Proficient would be given for that standard until it was properly completed.

The results were phenomenal! After the initial shock of the first test, on which everyone had at least one area where they were not proficient, the students quickly caught on that they had to show work or they would not pass the standard. Overnight, I was getting the full complete answers I had been begging the kids to give me.

The department created pacing charts and common assessments aligned to the curriculum standards so that teachers could gauge their instruction to the program recommendations. They also figured out a way to use their traditional gradebook program to allow them to input all assignments and assessments by standards. The math supervisor, Ron Wence, describes the student achievement gains:

Our department needed to make a change. Our department data indicated that students were generally averaging a marking period grade of 15 points higher than their final exam grade. This means that a student who got an 80 for the marking period typically would get a 65 on the final exam.

Last year, we began grading to our math standards in three courses (Algebra I, Geometry, and Algebra II Concepts & Applications). We had five teachers teaching these courses and each of them used a slightly different method even though the basics were the same.

Since we began grading to standards, the average exam grade is now three points higher than the marking period grade.

In order to gather data, the final exam is the same as the one that was given prior to students being graded to standards. So what does this mean? Are marking period grades going down, or exam grades going up? The average marking period grade has remained about the same at 84 while the final exam has risen from 68 to 87.

Ron and Betsy both state that their goal was to change assessment to impact student learning. Teachers share the common assessments, but more importantly, share the belief that all students are expected to reach a basic level of proficiency on the standards. A student can no longer pass a test and score an 85 percent and not know anything about one of the important topics on the test. They are required to obtain proficiency on all standards before their test is considered completed. All students, even resource room students, are expected to reach a certain level of proficiency on the same assessments.

One of the concerns that teachers have is that the emphasis of standards-based grading is to improve achievement for lower performing students. Ron's math department found that the top students in the class are still earning similar grades, but now say that they have to work harder to earn those grades and that they feel like they learned a lot more. The students who refuse to do any assignments are fewer in number. The most significant impact comes with the group of students that average a C or lower. Many of them are now B students, both during the marking period and on the exam. Those students now seem motivated to persevere and keep working, instead of just accepting a 70 just to get by.

In Ron and Betsy's department, the process of aligning math assessments to the standards to drastically improve feedback worked, but in other subject areas, teachers find that they need to change more than just the assessments. In the case of the English department, teachers changed their gradebooks because although teachers use the same standards, they were less likely to use the same assessments.

## PAUSE TO REFLECT

How does the math department experience compare to your own? Are your math standards acceptable and, if not, would the teachers consider improving the feedback by aligning the assessments to the standards?

## CHANGING GRADING HABITS

Grading habits are hard to change. For secondary teachers, the point and percentage system is so ingrained that even when they read convincing research or advice from experts such as Doug Reeves or Ken O'Connor, they have difficulty changing their habits. Elementary teachers tend not to keep gradebooks and eschew most suggestions that they evaluate students. Putting history and the habits aside, the fact is that current grading practices provide students with verification of their performances on tasks, but do not provide the informational feedback for improving on topics.

In *Developing Grading and Reporting Systems for Student Learning,* Guskey and Bailey (2001) explore how grading impacts student achievement by retelling a 1958 classic study by Page on grading. Some students received just the score, some received standard comments, and some students received individualized comments. On the next test, student scores increased for those who received specific comments. The researchers concluded that while grades "might not be essential for teaching and learning, grading can be used in positive ways to enhance students' achievement and performance," and "the positive effects can be gained with relatively little effort on the part of the teachers" (p. 29).

The English and math departments in the examples in this chapter approached grading as a feedback issue, expecting that if they changed their traditional grading habits then the result would be improved learning. They note positively that the hype and resistance to grading evaporates with standards-based feedback to students because better feedback from teachers works to accelerate achievement for all learners, particularly the unmotivated learners.

---

### PAUSE TO REFLECT

What are the assessment, grading, and record-keeping practices that your school uses or has tried to change to improve learning?

---

## FEEDBACK IN LARGE CLASSES

As a music educator, Jeremy Little admitted that one of the challenges he faced every day was the stark reality of teaching sixty students at varying skill levels the same music at the same time.

> Not only do we all need to learn the music together, we eventually need to perform it (not merely together, but at the exact moment, measure by measure, word by word).

This challenge is compounded by the fact that, although I give feedback on quite a regular basis, it is general. In fact, I would say that we music educators are "pioneers" of feedback: in a normal rehearsal we are constantly listening, analyzing the sound, and then giving timely and relevant feedback in order for the ensemble to improve. However, the nature of that feedback sometimes is quite generic (e.g., "Tenors, you are flat. Please use more breath energy to keep the higher notes in tune"). While that particular bit of feedback is often times helpful, what if only two of the ten tenors were actually flat? If all of them actually listened to my direction, I would now have two persons in tune and eight others pushing the line sharp!

Jeremy was clear that this kind of feedback for large group ensembles remains necessary, but in his personal journey to improve feedback to students to help them improve, he devised a more individualized feedback process into his classroom instruction that increased both student and ensemble performances.

Jeremy created a curriculum document and forms for students to be able to know and do. He asked students to evaluate their own progress toward each specific goal every week, usually only two or three goals per week. (See Figures 5.4 and 5.5.)

Once Jeremy became accustomed to weaving the goals into his lessons, students got into the habit of focusing on these specific goals and charting their own progress (and that of the class as a whole) each week. Because of the number of students, the student goal accounting templates did double-duty; they also substituted as teacher scoring templates since he scores alongside their scores.

What Jeremy described as the most surprising part of the process came after he started reading student responses (on topics

**Figure 5.4** Jeremy Little Singing Assessment

| Singing Assessment<br>Title_____ | Quarter 1     2     3<br>Title_____ |
|---|---|
| ☐ *Tone Quality*<br>☐ Consistent/appropriately focused<br>☐ Warm/rich/ringing<br>☐ Open throat, lifted soft palette<br>☐ Supported, connected sound<br>☐ Closet throat, low soft palette<br>☐ Unsupported, unconnected sound<br>☐ Nasal/forced/constricted<br>☐ Passagio/register issues<br>☐ Inconsistent: depth, placement, or vocal energy | ☐ *Tone Quality*<br>☐ Consistent/appropriately focused<br>☐ Warm/rich/ringing<br>☐ Open throat, lifted soft palette<br>☐ Supported, connected sound<br>☐ Closet throat, low soft palette<br>☐ Unsupported, unconnected sound<br>☐ Nasal/forced/constricted<br>☐ Passagio/register issues<br>☐ Inconsistent: depth, placement, or vocal energy |
| ☐ *Pitch*<br>☐ Accurate pitches/intonation<br>☐ Scooping/sliding/following<br>☐ Inaccurate pitches:<br>☐ Intonation problems: flat/sharp? where? | ☐ *Pitch*<br>☐ Accurate pitches/intonation<br>☐ Scooping/sliding/following<br>☐ Inaccurate pitches:<br>☐ Intonation problems: flat/sharp? where? |
| ☐ *Rhythm*<br>☐ Accurate rhythms/pulse<br>☐ Inaccurate rhythms<br>☐ Delaying beat/following<br>☐ Pulse problems: where? | ☐ *Rhythm*<br>☐ Accurate rhythms/pulse<br>☐ Inaccurate rhythms<br>☐ Delaying beat/following<br>☐ Pulse problems: where? |
| ☐ *Diction*<br>☐ Crisp, audible, precise<br>☐ Sloppy/mumbled/imprecise | ☐ *Diction*<br>☐ Crisp, audible, precise<br>☐ Sloppy, mumbled, imprecise |
| ☐ *Breath Energy*<br>☐ Deep/expansive breaths<br>☐ Steady airflow, energized<br>☐ Shallow breathing<br>☐ Many catch breaths<br>☐ Unsteady/unsupported airflow | ☐ *Breath Energy*<br>☐ Deep/expansive breaths<br>☐ Steady airflow, energized<br>☐ Shallow breathing<br>☐ Many catch breaths<br>☐ Unsteady/unsupported airflow |
| ☐ *Musicality/Expression*<br>☐ Performs with:<br>   • Excellent style and nuance<br>   • Some style and/or nuance<br>   • No style, everything is the same | ☐ *Musicality/Expression*<br>☐ Performs with:<br>   • Excellent style and nuance<br>   • Some style and/or nuance<br>   • No style, everything is the same |
| ☐ Overall, I did this well:<br><br>☐ Overall, I need to work on:<br><br>**Overall Grade** _____ | ☐ Overall, I did this well:<br><br>☐ Overall, I need to work on:<br><br>**Overall Grade** _____ |

Name _____

1. How well did I prepare?

2. What (specifically) was challenging to me in this song?

3. How does this performance rate in comparison to the best that I can do or have done?

4. How have I displayed growth and musical learning from:
   - The last singing assessment?

   - The beginning of the year?

Procedure: Students record themselves using a digital voice recorder. We have thirty students sing at a time, while the other thirty hold the music. Those who recorded then find a private spot and listen to their own performance and analyze or critique themselves according to the checklist. For each category, they score an overall 4, 3, 2, or 1 and write a plus or minus next to the check boxes they felt described their performance. They may add comments underneath each category. Students also fill out the right-hand column.

Afterwards, I listen to each performance and score and comment on each category so the students can see my scores and comments directly next to theirs.

We do three of these per quarter.

**Figure 5.5**   Jeremy Little Singing Assessment for Individual and
Ensemble

| Date _____ | | Name _____ |
|---|---|---|
| C = Class Effort | I = Individual Effort | U = Understanding |
| **Learning Targets** | | **Comments** |
| _____ | C | |
| _____ | I | |
| _____ | U | |

ranging from vocal production, to music reading, to analyzing a piece, to their own work ethic throughout the rehearsal).

Two incredible things happened. First, I was able to dialogue with every student about problems, concerns, and progress toward a specific goal on an individual level. We were able to have a prolonged, weekly conversation, and work together to find solutions or dialogue about murky points that were specific to their learning at that time. Second, I was able to alter my teaching when I saw trends in the class, specifically when many students commented that this point was unclear, or when some lesson went particularly well. It was as if I had a magical stethoscope to continually check on the progress of each of my "patients" every week.

Jeremy found the standards-based feedback to be so powerful that he combined it with technology.

After we've learned a particular section of a song, each member of the class will sing that section into a digital voice recorder. However, to make this truly authentic, everyone sings at the same time, but the recorders pick up each individual student's performance. Students then listen to their own performance and using a rubric, score themselves, and comment on their preparation and execution of the section.

I then listen to each student's performance and score and comment alongside theirs. After doing this five to seven times each semester, the students (and I) can see their progress, make adjustments for the future, and demonstrate growth.

When Jeremy describes the process, he indicates that it led to even more unintentional results, reminding us of the power of feedback as a hinge factor. After the first semester of doing this, he conducted a classroom discussion about the process of writing down the goals and commenting on them. While students generally thought it was a good idea (one brave soul: "We know it's like medicine; good for us, but we don't necessarily like it all the time"), they gave him feedback on how to teach to the goals even better. Among their suggestions were:

- Incorporate the specific goal into the lesson better, not just at the beginning and end of the period.
- Reduce the number of goals per week; focus on one or two really in-depth rather than trying to cover too much.
- Allow time for students' questions pertaining to that goal, as well as time for clarification or relevant side conversations related to the goal in question.
- Make sure the goal is well-worded and in clear language for students. Break down larger goals into smaller portions and eliminate overly wordy or unclear language.

After getting over the initial disappointment of not getting things right initially with this process, Jeremy realized that *that conversation* was what feedback is all about. The students gave him feedback based on how well they were doing.

> After making adjustments to the process after the first semester ended, we are beginning to learn and work toward specific goals now in the second semester. The process is hardly without bumps, but the bumps are the fun part . . . they tell us where we can improve.
> As a music educator, I find this process incredibly valuable: to work toward specific goals, constantly analyze and refine the product, make adjustments for future performances,

and generate a conversation (in one's own mind, between students themselves, or between students and the teacher) that shows evidence of learning and progress toward the goal. This process has allowed my students to become more critical thinkers, more independent creators of their own learning and growing, and better musicians and performers.

## PAUSE TO REFLECT

Examples like the music ensemble experience highlight the importance of including all teachers in the process of improving feedback regardless of class sizes. Considering other departments such as physical education or theatre, how can those teachers apply the strategies?

## WHAT MOTIVATES US

In his book *Drive: The Surprising Truth About What Motivates Us,* Daniel Pink (2009) shares what he believes to be the secret to high performance. He writes that "much of what we believe about the subject [motivation] just isn't so" (p. 9). Drawing on decades of scientific research on human motivation, Pink challenges us to consider three motivation theories he names 1.0, 2.0, and 3.0. The first (1.0), he argues, is our biological urges and our drive to survive. Then Motivation 2.0 dominated the landscape with the familiar carrots and sticks psychology, evident in most businesses. Today, however, he notes that jobs are far more interesting than in the early 1900s and that moving from an industrial to a conceptual age, the motivators in the new theory (3.0) will need to change. Pink notes that while carrots and sticks worked successfully in the twentieth century, the motivational theory today needs to change along with the demands of the times.

In *Drive,* Pink examines the self-determination theory (3.0) with three elements of true motivation: autonomy, mastery, and purpose. He suggests that some of the previous Motivation 2.0 is still necessary, but to move ahead, one needs to consider new methods that include greater flexibility to the individual to create and innovate. Considering Pink's discussion about Motivation 2.0 and 3.0, it seems that the examples of giving feedback by standards by walking around, using standards-based electronic record keeping, and deliberately aligning assessments to standards for purposes of improvement reflect the more contemporary motivation model for the students and the teachers.

In each of the cases, feedback was the hinge factor for improvement. The teachers changed their habits to give better feedback to students during class, sometimes called formative assessment or assessment during learning. The teacher became motivated in turn by the student feedback, recognizing the need to make changes for their instruction and assessment. As a result, the unmotivated students became more engaged and all learners learned ways to seek and use feedback to make improvement.

## PAUSE TO REFLECT

How do you perceive the timing and frequency of feedback that you give to students today? Would "walking around" with a scoring roster improve that feedback?

Without a software program, how can teachers still prepare and provide for standards-based feedback to students?

What process, individual or by department or grade level, would your school need to use to prepare the assessments to provide standards-based feedback to students?

How would the process of providing better feedback impact your technology initiatives?

# CHAPTER SIX

# FEEDBACK CHANGED MY TEACHING

---

A fter fifteen years, Frank Korb said he had that uneasy "Something's not right in Denmark" kind of feeling about teaching. He thought that his teaching was fine, he said, but not all of his students were performing well, or at least what he perceived as being commensurate with his efforts. When we started to talk about feedback, he said that was what he and other art teachers did best. But, he was open to new ideas.

With Frank, as with any teacher, I suggested increasing feedback in practical ways by introducing the tools in this order:

1. *Student Goal Accounting Templates:* feedback to self

2. *Turn-and-Talk With Observation Charts:* peer feedback and teaching

3. *Interactive Notebooks:* peer and teacher feedback

4. *Standards-Based Grading:* teacher feedback

# EXCEPT

"Except . . ." he responded aloud. At first it seemed like he was going to tick each one off the list, noting that art teachers already give lots of feedback to students. But instead, he thoughtfully added:

1. *Student Goal Accounting Templates.* "Art teachers already do that, except that we don't ask the students to write it down."

2. *Turn-and-Talk With Observation Charts.* "Art teachers already do that, except we don't ask students to maximize all sources of feedback in the room."

3. *Interactive Notebooks.* "Art teachers already do that, except that we call them sketchbooks and they don't use them in class; they are homework."

4. *Standards-Based Grading.* "Art teachers already do that, except I have made up my own standards for all of these years."

Frank taught me how important it is to listen to a teacher confirm that he is already doing something, *except.* . . .

*Except* gave us the starting point to acknowledge what he was doing successfully in order to meet many students' needs and also manage the materials, content, and unpredictability of an art teacher's world. *Except* became the mantra for how he could explain that, despite his great lesson delivery and assessment, a few tell-tale students did not perform well, and how managing feedback through student self-regulation, peer teaching, and teacher classroom feedback could improve engagement and achievement.

**PAUSE TO REFLECT**

When Frank realized the *except* of his own practices, he began to systematically work to improve learning. Have you noticed any *excepts* as you have read through the discussion about feedback?

## THE HOW, NOT THE WHAT

Frank looks back on the past eight months of the school year and admits that this year he changed his teaching so that his students would learn better. He marvels, "I'm an art teacher. For years people have complimented me on changing what I do each semester because I'm so creative. This year I actually I stopped changing the *what* and started changing the *how*. Honestly, it's because this year I changed my teaching for the students and not for myself."

When Frank began his work on the four techniques, coaching involved confirming what he did (sincerely posting state standards on the board because he was told to do so by the principal) and finding the "flip," such as posting standards with the intent of having students interact with the goals. Frank realized that he had always considered curriculum as *his units* in which *he needed to cover* material in a certain amount of time, as opposed to the curriculum standards or targets that a student would know and be able to do. He wrote:

Since I shifted my perspective to becoming very aware of all of my students receiving feedback, I have seen student engagement increase because of some pretty dramatic changes I made in my preparation for each class and classroom presentation techniques. In particular I am observing stronger attention being paid to the lectures, better note taking, and more conversation during class. Students also engage with a wider variety of their classmates, taking responsibility for their own behaviors and actions, and assuming a sense of ownership in their own understanding.

The biggest change I have made is that I start each week, day, and class period with clear and concise goal setting—for the students. While it was a challenge for me to switch from making weekly lesson plans to daily plans, I know that it is worth my time.

The change Frank describes is that in the past, he wrote a "goal" in the lesson plan for himself, the teacher, with the corresponding tasks he wanted students to complete, with long arrows that extended over a number of days. The goals, for example, read:

Visit the idea of chiaroscuro (from light to dark), using worksheets and images from past students. Begin the process of drawing out portraits; finish making photographs to create the self-portrait form; continue the process of building and preparing canvases.

To increase feedback to the students in a more methodical way, we separated his "teaching" goals from the student goals. First we asked, what is the student supposed to know and be able to do (using standards as shown in Figure 6.1)?

When we approached the goal setting this way, Frank realized that the topic or project was "self-portraits" but the visual arts standards could be unpacked to provide goals for learners for daily instruction and formative assessment. The students could sketch, for example, continuously receiving feedback about conceiving and creating the work of art. And they could read about and understand light and dark as a way to understand how to improve on self-portrait techniques.

**Figure 6.1** Self-portrait

| |
|---|
| Understand and apply media, techniques, and processes with skill, confidence, and sensitivity.<br><br>• Light and dark<br>• True form |
| Conceive and create works of visual art that demonstrate an understanding of how their ideas relate to the media, techniques, and processes they use.<br><br>• Drawing out—measurements<br>• Sketches<br>• Photographs<br>• Finishing |
| Initiate, define, and solve challenging visual arts problems.<br><br>• Canvas preparation<br>• Presentation of portrait |

Second, as Frank planned daily lessons within his unit, he realized that the "teacher goals" were the instruction: providing a lecture on chiaroscuro using video clips and images created by previous students.

Breaking my daily routine into teacher goals and student goals has made me think more carefully about the planning and delivery of information. Beginning each class period by presenting the visual arts goals for students helps them know what I am expecting of them during that period and what they can do better as a result of the time in class. What used to be a loose lesson plan for days of working on art works, has become explicit direction toward what I intend for them to understand and be able to do to make art.

Now I can emphasize process over product. I thought I was doing it before; now I know I am.

Once we separated teacher goals from student goals, Frank began to see clearly that each daily lesson was an opportunity for him to plan for ways for students to seek feedback to become more proficient on the standards. To summarize, Frank observed that some students performed well already (positive deviants), and feedback (invisible in plain sight) could be better if he changed (flipped) his goal setting to separate the teacher goals from the student goals.

Performance in class hinged on the students receiving feedback about the standards from the teacher, but also from their peers and through reflection.

The amount of feedback that my students are receiving has changed dramatically as I have changed my classroom techniques. While I have always walked around and commented on the work, I have started approaching the students in a more supportive, positive way, and with the visual arts goals more intentionally.

I make certain that my feedback is not simply "fluff" but is rather specific to the criteria. Even when my remarks have been critical, the response from the students has been wonderfully positive. The student ownership of behavior or lack of progress, and even apparent understanding of the success and unsuccessful aspects of their works, has improved.

Frank, who said that he was giving feedback already, was open to changing some of his habits. Once he unpacked the goals for that set of lessons, he realized that he would commit to the same for the rest of the year. He introduced the goal accounting templates first and then started to make the other changes to his teaching.

Casual peer conversations, turn-and-talks, became deliberately punctuated moments during lectures, extending to purposeful feedback-seeking on the part of the students. The sketchbook that once had been homework (and often not truly practice) transformed into complex note taking and true sketch practice. And, Frank began to track student progress by the standards as a way to give constructive feedback.

## PAUSE TO REFLECT

Frank, an art teacher, states that many teachers in the performing arts believe that they already use feedback as a powerful tool. In what ways could you describe to them how Frank changed his teaching to increase learning?

## TWENTY-FIRST CENTURY FEEDBACK

Over the course of the year, I coached Frank without ever going into his classroom because he lives in a different state. With cell phones, Skype, his class website, e-mail, and some video, Frank and I worked together side-by-side. Realizing that coaching was iterative and could transform his teaching if he sought feedback, we worked by breaking down the barriers of time and space.

The importance of this experience to both of us emphasizes the power of feedback. Ten years ago, we might have talked after a conference, two days later fallen into our routines, and a year later wished we had followed up with our commitment to make changes.

When we met, we exchanged e-mails. He sent me a lesson and asked a question. Soon the e-mails became weekly and evolved into a Skype call to clarify and share computer screens. Frank sent video clips of his delivery. When Frank began to use his website to post the goals and original work, it gave him feedback that galvanized the opportunity to share any time.

After a year, Frank started to coach many other teachers, informally, electronically, generously listening to teachers and giving advice about how to increase engagement. And few of them ever will be close enough to enter his classroom in person. Looking back, Frank made the small changes to his habits that resulted in strong gains for learners. In the process, he became a positive deviant for other art teachers.

## YOU DON'T NEED FEEDBACK
## UNTIL YOU NEED FEEDBACK

LaKeisha Newberry, middle school teacher, on the other hand, said she was fine. As is the case in many districts, she attended an ongoing staff development class that met for six sessions during the course of the school year. At each session, teachers used the new information to troubleshoot their own lessons.

Reflecting on the first few sessions, LaKeisha said confidently that each time the suggestions and the research made sense and she could see how to incorporate the changes into her lessons.

This year, I began intentionally using high-yield strategies because, to be honest, I didn't give them much thought before. I used them. I just didn't use them intentionally as a way to increase student engagement and achievement. Once I had a bit of training, I was surprised at how easy it was to use them and I was surprised at how much sense it made to organize my lessons for students to maximize feedback.

Each session, she had the opportunity to work with the math and literacy coaches and other teachers, but she really believed that she could learn enough from the classes to incorporate the ideas. Then, she hit the wall.

As a side note about working with adult learners, my lesson from LaKeisha was: "You don't need feedback until you need feedback." Sometimes when working with teachers, I find that they are not very interactive, and then one day, it clicks. Unlike working with students, teachers make their changes based on such a broad experience base, that often it takes two or three staff development sessions to marinate the information for the "need" to emerge. It gives a strong argument for shorter, more frequent staff development classes rather than one-day sessions.

After the fifth session, Lakeisha asked her coaches to help. When teaching daily lessons, the strategies such as the goal sheets, turn-and-talks, notebooks, and scoring made sense, but when she assigned the project she had successfully taught for a few years, she felt stymied. "This is where feedback came in," she said.

I began to rework a project that I had done with the students for the past two years. This project was an introduction to reading the play version of *A Diary of Anne Frank.* I asked the students to take close look at Billy Joel's song "We Didn't Start the Fire." We analyzed the song and discussed the theme. Then I asked the students to create their own personal version of the song. Day one of this project was set. The following three days would be research days. The students needed time to research political, social, sporting events, books, and movies, from the years of their own lives. In the past, when it came to research days we went to the lab and they would research. There was very little direct instruction from me.

"Last year and the year before, the project was fine, but this year I began to question myself before I taught it," she wrote.

"How are students going to receive feedback from themselves, peers, and others in the media center?" LaKeisha describes the moment when she realized she needed another perspective, or feedback from others.

I asked both the math and literacy facilitators in my building for help. They began researching and finding ideas for me. They were able to think outside the box. They gave new perspectives to a lesson I had taught the two previous years because they were a fresh set of eyes.

The new perspectives gave me great insight into my lesson, the strategies I tended to leave out, and new ways to pep up the days in which we seemed to be doing the same thing over and over. Due to the collaboration with my academic facilitators, my students gained a better understanding of how what we were creating related back to our goal. The students seemed more focused on their work and accomplishing their goals because I was now more focused on teaching and guiding them during the work days rather than leaving them to work on their own during a project.

## FEEDBACK FOR MYSELF

Frank and LaKeisha represent two examples of how important it is to consider the adult professional learner characteristics. Some teachers learn well in lectures, others with ongoing feedback, and some with very little interaction. Teachers, like any other person, can benefit from feedback to make improvement. As professionals, most of the teachers find ways that they can slightly adapt their existing practices, or ladle the soup differently.

## HINGES IN ACTION

Any performer can benefit from feedback. Because teachers focus on providing feedback opportunities for students, they may not realize how powerful feedback can shift their own teaching and assessing from skillful to outstanding.

Another teacher, Pat Carosello, surprised me yet again because her feedback needs came from herself. Pat teaches math. During the school year, Pat attended sessions and always seemed satisfied but never asked for help from me. At the end of the year, she approached me to say that her students were performing much better than any year previously (her supervisor confirmed the same). Then, she showed me a notebook.

Since I assumed it was going to be a student notebook, I expected to see the notes, organizers, and goal sheets. As I peered through the book, I realized that Pat had kept her own notebook that year (see Figure 6.2).

Pat said she did it for two reasons. First, she wanted to know what it felt like to the learners to have to sustain a notebook all year long and not lose it. Second, she wanted to be able to make corrections to lessons as she taught them so that she could avoid the mistakes in the next lesson or the next year.

Teachers do need feedback when they decide to make changes to their teaching habits in order to increase student engagement and achievement. Some teachers find benefit from peer tutoring, some need it when they need it, and teachers like Pat, need to be able to self-teach.

**Figure 6.2**   Pat Carosello's Notebook

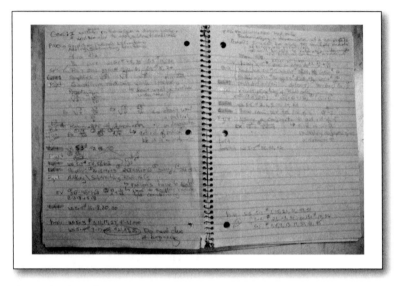

*Source:* Pat Carosello.

## EVERYBODY'S TALKING AT ME

Darlene Markle, middle school principal, said, "Two years ago, I received comments from the district office administrator who noted that during her walk-through observations, she saw that some of the students seemed disengaged during class." She continued:

> I knew that, but hearing it from another administrator motivated me to make some changes. For a few months, I went to classrooms to watch for myself. Until then, teachers knew that they could use the goal accounting templates and other strategies if they wanted to do so, but now, I insisted upon it. Looking back, I think the teachers must have felt oppressed by my presence. By monitoring, I was going to make it

happen; I could go into classrooms and tell them what was missing and how to change it.

As life happens for a middle school principal, parent meetings began to take up time, and I could not monitor so much, so I organized meetings for teachers to work on templates, cooperative learning, and interactive notebooks, and grading to the standards with the plan to implement schoolwide by the next year. Three months later, everyone was talking at me. Teachers wanted better curriculum documents and expected me to help them find them. Teachers wanted time to observe other classes and expected me to arrange for the logistics. Teachers wanted to read some books on instruction and for me to find books and videos. Teachers wanted to change their assessments. Teachers wanted. Teachers wanted.

Darlene will agree that it is all about the feedback, but when it comes to adult learners, it is complicated. She called one day to ask:

Have you ever read the book *The Tipping Point,* by Malcolm Gladwell? Well, it happened here. When I stopped trying to initiate the feedback to teachers to ensure that they were giving feedback to students, but instead, provided the tools, time for conversation, and multiple venues with the technical information about the research and strategies, it seemed like an avalanche happened. What started as a little activity has become a powerful movement, all directed at improving learning for every child.

Darlene's office changed from a place were no student or teacher ever wanted to go because they might be told to do something, to the turnstile office where teachers sought ways to find solutions for teaching tell-tale students.

## TELL-TALE STUDENTS, A HINGE
## FACTOR, AND POSITIVE DEVIANTS

Reflecting on the experiences shared in this chapter and from teachers' comments, it seems that the complicated and frustrating issue of increasing student achievement can be successfully addressed as long as you have some tell-tale students, a hinge factor, and a few positive deviants.

Most teachers have lived through a few of the waves of reform that include curriculum changes from outcomes to standards to the Common Core, and structural changes from modular schedules to blocks, and assessment changes from progressive assessment models to computer-based programs. We have also lived through various "education" presidents and governors. All of the structural and social changes have produced gains and changed according to the times, but the one constant over the past twenty years is that in every class a few students disengaged during the lesson for no apparent medical or psychological reason.

That tell-tale student, the warning that something is not working, motivates us to find a solution that has to be "invisible in plain sight." By recognizing feedback as the hinge factor that allows for efficient transfer of information from the teacher to the student, and back to the teacher again, we can continue to devise simple tools to ensure that it can happen methodically yet creatively, for any student at any grade level.

# REFERENCES AND RESOURCES

Agatston, A. (2003) *The South Beach diet.* Emmaus, PA: Rodale.

Ayers, I. (2007). *Super Crunchers.* New York: Bantam Books.

Black, P., & William, D. (1998). Inside the black box: Raising standards through classroom assessment. *Phi Delta Kappan, 80*(2), 139–148.

Doidge, N. (2007). *The brain that changes itself.* New York: Penguin Books.

Fullan, M. (2010). *Motion leadership: The skinny on becoming change savvy.* Thousand Oaks, CA: Corwin.

Gladwell, M. (2002). *The tipping point.* New York: Little, Brown.

Guskey, T., & Bailey, J. (2001). *Developing grading and reporting systems for student learning.* Thousand Oaks, CA: Corwin.

Hattie, J. (2009). *Visible learning: A synthesis of over 800 meta-analyses relating to achievement.* London: Routledge.

Hattie, J., & Timperley, H. (2007). The power of feedback. *Review of Educational Research, 77*(1), 81–112.

Kagan, S., & Kagan, M. (2009). *Kagan cooperative learning.* San Clemente, CA: Kagan.

Kulhavy, R. W., & Stock, W. A. (1989). Feedback in written instruction: The place of response certitude. *Educational Psychology Review, 1*(4), 279–308.

Locke, E., & Latham, G. (2002). Building a practically useful theory of goal setting. *The American Psychologist, 57*(9), 705–717. doi: 10.1037/0003–066X.57.9.705

Marzano, R. (2009). When students track their progress. *Educational Leadership, 67*(4) 86–87.

Marzano, R. J., Pickering, D. J., & Pollock, J. E. (2001). *Classroom instruction that works: Research-based strategies for increasing student achievement.* Alexandria, VA: Association for Supervision and Curriculum Development.

Mason, J., & Bruning. (2001). *Providing feedback in computer-based instruction: What the research tells us.* Retrieved from http://dwb.unl.edu/Edit/MB/MasonBruning.html

Mory, E. H. (1992). The use of informational feedback in instruction: Implications for future research. *Educational Technology Research and Development, 40*(3), 5–20.

Pascale, R., Sternin, J., & Sternin, M. (2010). *The power of positive deviance: How unlikely innovators solve the world's toughest problems.* Boston: Harvard Business Press.

Pink, D. (2009). *Drive: The surprising truth about what motivates us.* New York: Riverhead Books.

Pollock, J. E. (2007). *Improving student learning one teacher at a time.* Alexandria, VA: Association for Supervision and Curriculum Development.

Pollock, J. E., & Ford, S. M. (2009). *Improving student learning one principal at a time.* Alexandria, VA: Association for Supervision and Curriculum Development.

Popham, W. J. (2008). *Transformative assessment.* Alexandria, VA: Association for Supervision and Curriculum Development.

Ramachandran, V. S. (2011). *The tell-tale brain: A neuroscientist's quest for what makes us human.* London: W.W. Norton.

Stiggins, R. (2008). *Assessment manifesto.* Portland, OR: Educational Testing Service.

Wiggins, G. (2010, May 22). Feedback: How learning occurs. *Big Ideas.* Retrieved from http://www.authenticeducation.org

Willis, J. (2006). *Research-based strategies to ignite student learning.* Alexandria, VA: Association for Supervision and Curriculum Development.

# INDEX

# CORWIN

A SAGE Company

The Corwin logo—a raven striding across an open book—represents the union of courage and learning. Corwin is committed to improving education for all learners by publishing books and other professional development resources for those serving the field of PreK–12 education. By providing practical, hands-on materials, Corwin continues to carry out the promise of its motto: **"Helping Educators Do Their Work Better."**